WWW.100HAPPYDAYS4KIDS.COM

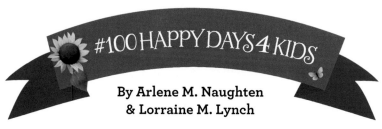

#100 HAPPY DAYS 4 KIDS

**By Arlene M. Naughten
& Lorraine M. Lynch**

www.100happydays4kids.com

In association with Sugru

Edited by Lorraine M. Lynch

ISBN no 978-1-78280-437-6 – #100happydays4kids

Design and layout by Siobhan Foody

SiobhanFoody.com

#100
HAPPY DAYS
4 KIDS

DEDICATIONS & ACKNOWLEDGMENTS

Lorraine M. Lynch

I dedicate this work to the force of maternal womanliness who is my mother, a lady who has unceasingly taken every effort to raise her children as best she could. After becoming a widow in her early twenties with four young children and no income, Mam did not have time to grieve, regret or long for anything because life went on and nappies needed to be changed. She re-married and went on to have three more children, to whom she has given her everything. Mam is why I never complain about the small things in life, why I have dedicated my life to promoting familial well-being and child development, and why I have so much respect for every mother and father out there 'doing their best'. She could not afford to bring us on holidays or give us birthday parties but she taught me the strength of education, the value of travel and the importance of independence, respect and honesty. This book is proof of your unfaltering commitment to your children, Mam, and that I did listen to you sometimes.

For my friends from Ireland, Korea and America who amaze me every day with their love and loyalty.

For Sinead who will still be giggling with me over a vino when we are ninety.

For Jimmy who gives me unconditional coffee, smiles, cheese, support and love.

For Eoin, Aoife and Roisin who have contributed more to this book than they know.

Arlene M. Naughten

For me, this book is dedicated to one of the greatest mothers I know, Helena, who is represented by the butterfly sitting proudly on the cover. Helena was taken from her mothering role after only twelve years, leaving behind a most wonderful legacy. In setting out to write this book, Helena had a special place in my heart and I wished for her to serve as an inspiration to others. Helena died with no regrets and her daughter lives on with the peace of mind that she received, from her mother, everything that she had to give, in the time they had together and, for that she is a lucky girl. There are many parents who are stripped from their role prematurely. For me, I see this as a constant reminder to give our children the absolute best we can in the time that we are blessed with having them. This book embraces that - it shows parents how to live every day by injecting something positive into the lives of their children, ensuring that they are being built upon emotionally to face the complexities of life and embracing these when they come along by utilising the strength in their hearts from the love and dedication of their parents.

I owe eternal gratitude to my family – my mother, father, husband, and my precious daughter, Cailín Éaoibheann – my girl of radiant beauty.

Introduction

THE idea for this book emerged directly from interactions with children and parents who all presented with the same type of needs. Children strive for secure attachments with their care givers, which in turn gives them the solid base to navigate their social worlds and explore their identities from. To enhance the way a children's development is supported, parents need to be equipped with fundamental parenting skills that rarely are described adequately to parents. The more children and families we have worked with in a therapeutic context, the more convinced we have become that simple communication, mindfulness and understanding within the family unit could have prevented a substantial amount of difficulties for children and young people.

Our combined experiences of years working with children and families, as well as qualitative and quantitative findings in psychological literature, have highlighted a marked increase in rates of anxiety, depression and related psychological difficulties. These manifest as a result of numerous 'modern' pressures, including changes in family structures, pressures of advertising and social media, higher rates of parental unemployment and subsequent mental ill-health, and lack of quality time spent together as a family unit. Alarmingly, research has shown that without therapeutic intervention, these conditions generally persist into adulthood. This book allows you to readily adopt therapeutic techniques into your family. Rather than postulate some new theory about how to be the perfect parent, we believe that parenting needs to go back to basics. It costs nothing and requires no extra effort, but the benefits are expansive.

The moment a parent understands that their child is a unique individual, rather than just their son or daughter, is an important one as it suddenly reframes how children should be treated. They deserve constant love, understanding, assurance, affection and respect because their worlds, languages, social skills and identities are still being constructed. Would you like to be woken up by a more dominant person who rushes you through your day and does not give you the chance to finish your activities, express your opinion or follow your own pursuits? How about being scolded and embarrassed in front of your friends until you cry and then being expected to self-soothe? When we really think about what our child's life is like, we begin to take our understanding to a new level.

This book will allow you to see how your child views you, what your child really feels about him/herself, how your child is progressing within their own social circles and what path your child follows when left to their own devices.

This book will allow you to see how your child views you, what your child really feels about him/herself, how your child is progressing within their own social circles and what path your child follows when left to their own devices. Rather than telling children how they should behave, we believe in leading by example. Rather than telling a child how they should play, we believe in providing children with the forum to create, explore and experiment at their own pace. Rather than telling kids that they can come to us with any problem, we believe in showing them that we are understanding, considerate and non-judgemental with the small things – in preparation for the big things. Telling someone you love them is one thing but making them feel loved is something they will never forget.

By following our one hundred simple steps, you will learn all about how to practice and teach effective communication, the importance of expressing emotions within a family, the value of being mindful in your family's daily life and a number of fundamental parenting skills to enhance your child's responsiveness. These are akin to methods therapists use with children in order to begin the healing process; however, nurturing your child before any difficulties acts as a protective mechanism. We have broken these down into one hundred easy-to-follow tasks such that parents can easily understand and implement the most effective psychological techniques.

We hope that you enjoy taking part in this important positive parenting movement as much as we have enjoyed creating it. #100happydays4kids has been a labour of love and has been designed specifically to improve children and familial well-being all over the world.

Today I will listen, really listen, to everything my child has to say

#activelistening

WHAT DO I NEED TO DO?

Every time your child calls you or comes up to talk to you today, take that as your cue to make this their happy day number one by doing the following: pause the task at hand, go down to your child's level and listen to whatever it is that your child wants to share with you. If it is a number of children that want your attention at the one time, take this opportunity to teach all of them the value of listening. Go down to the level of the child who approached you first and give them your undivided attention and then, do the same thing with each child individually. To ensure everyone feels as though they have been heard, simply repeat back what they have said to you. Once each child has been listened to, resume what you had been doing. Repeat this during the day each time your child approaches or calls you with something to tell you, remembering that every word your child utters is precious and provides you with a window to look into their inner world.

WHY AM I DOING THIS?

Listening to children has a wide range of benefits for your child, which apply from as soon as the child is born right into adulthood. The most important of these benefits is that you can increase your child's self-esteem as a result of them having their views heard and respected by adults.[1] Stemming from this, a child can learn new skills as their confidence levels grow. For example, you may see that children become more skilled at communicating in social situations and in voicing their views when with their peers. Listening to your children provides them with a forum to reflect on the thoughts and ideas they hold about the world and allows them to communicate their perceptions of the world, in a way that is meaningful to them.[2] Of course, there is also the possibility that being listened to may inspire your child to tell you about matters that are concerning them, for example, if someone is bullying them at school, if a stranger has approached them on the street, or if someone is doing something to them that they are not happy with.

FUNDAMENTAL PARENTING SKILL

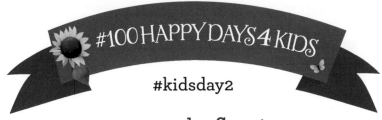

#parentalreflection

Take some time out to pause and look back at how you have been parenting your child – reflect on your strengths and areas for improvement

#parentalreflection

WHAT DO I NEED TO DO?

Take some time to yourself today to pause and reflect on how you have been parenting your children to date. Often, parents spending years raising their children before they look back and see how they actually fared. To reflect on your style, look back at the type of parenting you have engaged in. Ask yourself if you have adopted any particular style and look at the ways you communicate with your children, as well as the ways you have disciplined your children, and at how your overall parental approach has made you feel. In conducting this reflection, it is preferable to write your thoughts down, thus, forming a tangible means of reviewing your reflection outcomes at a later date. It may prove useful to add to this over time, tracking how things are changing in your parental engagements all the while and how this is contributing to a change within you.

WHY AM I DOING THIS?

Reflection is a useful learning tool as it helps us to stop and actually look at what we are doing. From here, we can pick out our particular values and begin to work on using these more frequently. We can also strategically identify the areas in which we could have done better or the areas that did not work out at all. In documenting the outcomes of your reflections, you are engaging in a process which studies reveal enhances benefits for both mental and physical health. This is the process of simply putting pen to paper and expressing your emotional difficulties.[3]

FUNDAMENTAL PARENTING SKILL

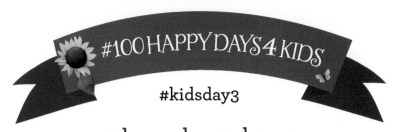

#kidsday3

#dancedancedance

Dance, dance, dance

#dancedancedance

WHAT DO I NEED TO DO?

Today, the clue is in the name. Whether you feel like spending an hour boogying in every room in the house or facilitating a fifteen-minute disco in the kitchen, the key today is for you and your child to throw a few moves to a funky beat. Your child may be surprised to see that Mammy or Daddy can act silly and you want for them to see you in this new way. It might also be a way you two had not communicated with one another before. It does not matter if you are not a very 'rhythmica' mover; the point here is that you MOVE. This can be done first thing in the morning, after dinner-time, or last thing before bed and is a simple exercise, which can be enjoyed by all the family. Have a ball!

WHY AM I DOING THIS?

The benefits of dance have been well-documented and range from physical fitness to increased endorphin (happy hormone) levels. However, research that has been done by social psychologists also suggests that moving in synchrony with your child, which is what happens when you are both listening to the same song, can actually strengthen the bond and attachment between the two dancers and result in increased cooperation.[4] Over time, increased cooperation promotes a higher level of relationship quality between parents and children.

ACTIVITY-BASED LEARNING

Checking in

#checkingin

WHAT DO I NEED TO DO?

A common practice in counselling with adults and children is to 'check in' with oneself a number of times during the day. This simple habit helps alleviate stress accumulating and allows you to notice patterns of negative thought or areas of anxiety that you might not have realized. As a result, you are asked to teach your child to check-in but are also encouraged to carry this task out yourself. It is so simple: you are asked to ask yourself five times throughout the day 'How are you doing?' Are you feeling tired, lonely, annoyed, amused, excited, sad, jealous, or anxious? Write it down. At these five times, your child is asked to do the same. If they are able to write this themselves, that is so much better but offer to help too. Younger children can be asked about how they feel and asked to explain what they mean when they say 'better' or 'angry'. You can either set your alarm to five times throughout the day or leave it to chance, but try to spread the times out as evenly as you can. In the evening time, look at your lists and have a chat about them.

WHY AM I DOING THIS?

Please feel free to carry out this experiment with your child on a longer time-frame, like a week or a month. You may begin to see a pattern after some time: more negative feelings in the evening or on Tuesdays; more positive feelings when your child is with you or when you are both at the swimming pool; or feelings of frustration around a certain activity, chore or person. You may begin to see that there are ways to alter your emotions such that you can both experience more positive emotions more often. You could find out what exactly it is about Tuesdays that leads to this negative mood and change it, or you could both choose to go swimming more often. It is this simple exercise of checking in that can highlight some missed but obvious clues to your child's overall mental health. This type of mindful practice results in a non-judgmental awareness that only comes from intentionally paying attention to unfolding experiences.[5]

INDEPENDENCE BUILDING

#kidsday5

#familymealtogether

Have a meal together as a family

#familymealtogether

WHAT DO I NEED TO DO?

The focus of today is on the family being together for a meal, rather than on the meal itself. However, it may be useful to pick a meal that you know is a family favorite and needs little tailoring for every member of the family to enjoy (including the cook). The more difficult part of this task is to plan for the family to be together at a time that is suitable for a meal. It can be any meal of the day – breakfast, lunch, dinner or supper. Just ensure that you are allowing at least half an hour for sitting together. It may require a parent coming home early from work, getting up earlier or coming home for lunch, but it is a sacrifice to be made for only one day. Be sure to include all children in this meal, even young babies who can simply be present at the dinner table. To really be 'together' for the meal time involves everyone being fully present, which is impossible with a phone, tablet, TV or any other such distraction, so ask that these devices be left out of the dining area for today. All that is left to do now is enjoy this time together!

WHY AM I DOING THIS?

The benefits of having a family meal have been firmly established for children of all ages. For teenagers, this simple activity has shown to result in a more positive mood,[6] a more positive future outlook,[7] and a reduced rate of depression and suicidal thoughts.[8] For school-age children, research indicates that the frequency of family meal-times is a better predictor of high achievement scores than time spent in school or time spent doing homework.[9] For young children, research indicates that they can learn more words from being present at family meal times than from parents reading directly to them.[10] Finally, more shared family meals have been shown to positively correlate with perceived family cohesion.[11]

FAMILY ATTACHMENT AND BONDING

#kidsday6

#smile

Smile

FUNDAMENTAL PARENTING SKILL

#smile

WHAT DO I NEED TO DO?

Hopefully, the task today will be a familiar one. The clue is in the name – smile! For some, this goes without saying but, for others, it may take paying attention to your smile to highlight how much more time we could spend doing this. You are not being asked to wear a painful fake smile for most of the day; rather, to greet your child with a warm smile, answer their questions with a smile, and provide a smile during all interactions. Notice how you can have more positive relations just by altering this one aspect of your life. Often, smiling follows the tenets of 'fake it 'til you make it', in that you will genuinely want to smile more after some practice.

WHY AM I DOING THIS?

Every parent wants to see their child happy and content, and the best way of noticing whether this is so is by noticing how much the child smiles. By altering this one simple habit, parents can increase the amount of time their child spends smiling. Research has shown young children are able to precisely copy the facial expression of others[12] and that even new-born babies have the natural ability to reflect their own mother's smile.[13] This has been found to be an ability that is engrained in the brain of the young child, rather that something that is learned.[14] Thus, it makes logical sense that, with very little effort required, the more a mother smiles at her baby, the more the baby smiles.

#kidsday7

#pajamaparty

Pajama party

#pajamaparty

WHAT DO I NEED TO DO?

Not very much today, and that is okay too! The point of the exercise today is for you and your child to really take the day and unwind fully and totally in your pajamas, allowing as much time as possible for art, games and relaxing in front of the fire. You are asked to not be concerned about cleaning, commitments, what the neighbors will think, or the errand you forgot the run. The likelihood is that if it was detrimentally important, you would have run it yesterday knowing that a Pajama Party was your task for today, or that it can wait until tomorrow. We normally associate children's games with chaos and noise but today you are asked to join in on the fun and PLAY like a child. You will be surprised how much fun being a child and forgetting about your adult responsibilities can be. Your child will be all the better for spending some down-time with Mammy/Daddy.

WHY AM I DOING THIS?

Playing is an activity we associate with children and, often, we regard it as something they should do with other children. However, adults need to have time to play also, although we tend to frame it in a different way, for example, bowling, playing soccer or dancing. Fundamentally, this is the same concept and playing is just as important for adults as it has the same benefits – social interaction, release of endorphins (happy hormones) and reduction of stress. Spending your day in your pajamas with your child is worthwhile on a number of levels; however, in these modern times, a primary focus for parents needs to be reducing technology and spending as much quality time with our children as we can in an environment which is free from stress and over-stimulation. This is due to the fact that stress has so many detrimental long-terms ramifications on child and adolescent psychology.[15]

ACTIVITY-BASED LEARNING

#kidsday8

#musicwakeup

Music
wake-up

#musicwakeup

WHAT DO I NEED TO DO?

Morning times can often be a real struggle for both parents and children, and is often considered a time of strict routine, with no elements of fun. Let's shake it up! Today, you are asked as a loving kind parent to wake your child up and immediately play his/her favorite music loudly for all to enjoy. Better still, why not create a playlist of all of your family's favorites? Naturally, elements of dance can also be incorporated into this task but the point is to experience your usual routine while positive happy music is playing in the background, in order to set yourself and your child up for the day and create some happy memories. Do not forget to add some of your own favorites so you can feel the benefits for the rest of the day too.

WHY AM I DOING THIS?

The positive effects of music have been widely cited in psychology and health research literature as having powerful effects on socio-emotional processes (having fun with friends), cognitive status (feeling more alert), and mood (feeling happy) and, as a result, actually contribute to healing.[16] It requires almost no effort, is super-beneficial for your health and is free! The positive powers of music is extensive as it has been shown to produce significant positive effects on patients with motor difficulties,[17] asthma[18] and those undergoing surgical procedures.[19] Any form of positive or relaxing music can be used, as personal feelings about the music and preferred styles have been shown to actually have very little effect on the response.[20]

FAMILY ATTACHMENT AND BONDING

Today, I will give my child one hour of non-directed play

#playityourway

WHAT DO I NEED TO DO?

Set aside an hour per child where you are fully available to simply play. During this hour, engage in non-directed play and let your child guide you in every way. Let your child know that you are there for an hour to play whatever they want and that it is completely up to them what and how you both play. During this time, follow your child's lead and ask your child what your role should be as the play progresses. If you are painting, ask your child would they like you to paint the same picture with them or for you to paint on a separate page. At then minutes to the end, give your child a warning that it will be ending in ten minutes, and repeat this at five minutes and at one minute so they know the play session is ending and that you must return to making your own decisions after that.

WHY AM I DOING THIS?

Virginia Axline pioneered a method of counselling children and coined the approach 'non-directive' therapeutic play, now commonly referred to as Child-Centered Play Therapy.[21] In this approach, a number of principles are followed to allow the play to have therapeutic benefits for the child. To do this, you need to accept where the child is at in that present moment, be warm in your engagements, encourage permissiveness so they feel free to express themselves fully, permit them to make their own choices in the play, remain fully non-directive in play, conduct, and conversation, and stay at the pace set by the child. By adopting these principles, you are likely to mirror some of the benefits that can be achieved from play therapy. Its effectiveness as a developmentally-responsive tool for children exhibiting a range of mental health concerns is support by a wide body of research spanning over seven decades.[22]

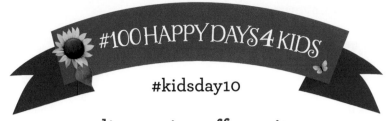

#100 HAPPY DAYS 4 KIDS

#kidsday10

#discussionoffavorites

Discussion of favorites

#discussionoffavorites

WHAT DO I NEED TO DO?

Have you ever had a conversation where you sat down with your child and really tried to get to know their personalities? We often sit with friends and talk about things we like to do and wear, and places we like to go. Today, you are asked to discuss both of your favorite objects, people, places and concepts with your child. This conversation can be had during play, on a journey in a car or over lunch, and is best had when you are both able to make and maintain eye-contact. Therefore, take time out from all activities when there can be no interruptions, ask your child about their favorites and ask them WHY. For each of these, take the time to tell your child about your favorites too. You may learn something new, think of ways to incorporate their favorites into your home, or be surprised by things you both have in common.

WHY AM I DOING THIS?

This very simple task is designed to encourage you to start flexing that 'communication muscle'. Getting to know your child is not something that can be done in one day but is something that is chipped away at every day. Aside from that, you and your child are both constantly changing so every effort needs to be made to check in with who your child is, what their thoughts are and how they are feeling. Your child is also learning new things, meeting new people and seeing new sights every day and this leads to them having new questions, emotions and, of course, favorites. It is this 'fluidity' of psychological development that often results in parents feeling distanced from their child. Remember that effective communication between individuals produces clarity[23] and co-creates an impression of mutual meaning.[24]

FUNDAMENTAL PARENTING SKILL

#100 HAPPY DAYS 4 KIDS

#kidsday11

#fourseasonsspring

Four seasons - Spring

#fourseasonsspring

WHAT DO I NEED TO DO?

Today, things will get creative as we mix the different mediums or expressions of emotions, music and art. As always, you are encouraged to join in but attempt to make this time private and personal, so the final painting really is that of your child's mind. Vivaldi's Four Seasons has been chosen as it includes four pieces of music which relate to the different seasons and, as such, may be very different from one another. Today, we will focus on the first movement of Spring (Allegro). You are asked to play this for your child once while they are in a relaxed position, explain to them that it is a piece of music about Spring-time and ask them to think about (but not tell you) what is going on in their imagination. Once they have attended to this, you are asked to provide paint and paper, ask your child to paint what they see and explain that you will play the same piece of music again during their painting to help them remember. Repeat the music as many times as they need. It is best if the child can only hear the music and not see any images relating to the music, as it might influence their art.

WHY AM I DOING THIS?

Many arts experiences which occur in mainstream education facilities include specific direction by teachers, are focused on the appearance of the end-product, and do not represent the true experience of what art is.[25] Although referred to as arts experiences by early childhood practitioners, this type of directed work does not culminate in any real development of expressive talents,[26] artistic appreciation,[27] or cognition.[28] However, allowing a child to listen to the musical art-form, with very little information pertaining to what it is about, allows them to become involved in the process of imaginative and creative art, without being influenced by any standards or comparison.

ACTIVITY-BASED LEARNING

Today, I will take the first step towards making bedtime a really positive part of my child's day

#timeforsleep

WHAT DO I NEED TO DO?

As you proceed through the happy days for kids, you will meet a number of days that focus on night-time. These are steps designed to make your child's bed-time experience the best it can be. The first of these steps is to give this nurturing part of the day sufficient time to follow the pace of the child and omit the stress that can easily upset your child, for example, rushing the process. The eventual aim is to allow for two hours preparation for sleep-time for your child but, for today, allow one hour and this will be built upon during later steps. Therefore, for today, if you want your child to be asleep by eight o'clock, start the preparation for sleep process at seven o'clock.

WHY AM I DOING THIS?

There are two reasons for doing this: the first is so your child has started the bed-time routine before they get over-tired and the second is such that your child's last feeling before sleep is a positive one, rather than a feeling of anxiety. When a child becomes over-tired, a hormone called cortisol is released in the brain of the child. This hormone-release is a reaction to stress in the child's body, caused by the body's need to sleep. In response to the need of the body not being met, this hormone will kick in to sustain the body's wakefulness.[29] Cortisol is a steroid hormone, which makes it far more difficult for us to sleep, and can also result in the child waking periodically during the night. Studies reviewing bed-time problems in children have found that an overwhelming majority of children respond favorably to a positive approach at bed-time and that this also improves child and family well-being.[30]

FAMILY ATTACHMENT AND BONDING

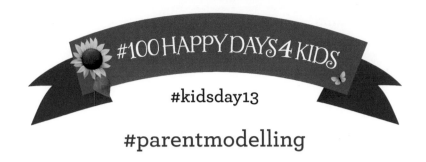

#parentmodelling

Parental modelling

#parentmodelling

WHAT DO I NEED TO DO?

You need to be the person that you want your child to be. This is not an easy task but, by simply acting in the way you want your child to, you are providing them with a deep learning experience. This is the same premise for small interactions like saying 'Please' and 'Thank you', to more complex interactions like working out a difference of opinion. Model the basics by saying 'Please' when you ask your child for something and 'Thank you' when they give you something. Remember that this is a much different process than telling a child to use their manners. Under these circumstances, they may say it because they were asked to, but they will not learn it as a natural behavior. Through the process of modelling, the child will inherently integrate this habit into their understanding of the world.

WHY AM I DOING THIS?

In social learning theory,[31] shows how children learn by observing the interactions and behaviors of their models. In turn, children encode these behaviors and imitate them when an appropriate situation arises. It is through this process that negative behaviors are often reinforced so easily. When a child observes their model shouting, they learn to shout themselves and will then frequently shout at their peers or at their family members when similar situations arise. Modelling appropriate behavior yourself will influence your child to behave in a much more positive way.

INDEPENDENCE BUILDING

I will tell my child I love them as many times as I can today

#iloveyoukid

WHAT DO I NEED TO DO?

Today is your day to convey your unabashed feelings of adoration to your child. As soon as your child wakes up, what a wonderful way to start their day. Say it first thing in the morning, as you send them off to school, when you collect them, when you sit for a movie in the evening, and last thing before they go to sleep. Why not put a note in their lunchbox or draw them a picture to put on their wall? Make sure your tone is genuine and heartfelt. Sometimes, telling your child you love them can be more difficult as they get older; however, it is equally as important for the teenager to know they are loved in this uncertain and awkward stage in life. The point of this exercise is for the child to feel loved. Sometimes, it goes without saying or we are too busy or shy to openly express our feelings. However, think back to the first time you fell in love with your child and remember all the milestones along the way that made you appreciate this little person coming into your life. Think of the times they made you laugh and of how you feel when you see him/her laughing. Consider all their little quirks, what makes them unique, and how they have changed you as a person.

WHY AM I DOING THIS?

There is no limit on how many times a person can feel as though or be told they are loved. Parental expressions of love and affection, such as hugging and kissing, are a vital part of a child's healthy development and are associated with low levels of behavioral difficulties, such as hitting and kicking.[32] This type of affection is also related to more effective regulation of emotions, which is due to the child having a better ability and more resources to cope with negative situations and feelings.[33] For example, they may feel more comfortable and less insecure in new situations just knowing and feeling they are completely loved.

FUNDAMENTAL PARENTING SKILL

#kidsday15

#thejoysofnature

Today, I will show my child how to experience the joys of nature

#thejoysofnature

WHAT DO I NEED TO DO?

Put aside an hour or two of your day to dedicate to being outside with your children and showing them how fun nature can be. This day is not about playing outside with toys or in structured sport but rather the focus is on interacting with nature. One way that you might do this is to go to a park with your child and to get them interested in exploring all of the gifts of nature to be found in the park. You could guide them in a treasure hunt by naming out a list of items that they must find in the park and remember that they must collect every item on the list. Such items may be different colored leaves, a piece of grass, a flower, a petal, a stone, a stick and a piece of moss. Later on that day, you can help your child relive the memories of the activity by bringing home the items found and helping your child to stick them on to a cardboard background with glue or sticky tape and creating a picture of their memory.

WHY AM I DOING THIS?

We are living in an age where families tend to have limited opportunities to spend time outdoors simply connecting with nature. This has inspired a body of scientific research which has resulted in the documentation of the benefits of connecting with nature. Collectively, this body of research shows that children's social, psychological, academic and physical health is positively impacted upon when they have daily contact with nature. Engaging with nature has an array of potential benefits for both nature and for individual health and well-being. Simply being outside and learning to be comfortable in a variety of weather conditions can inspire children to walk or cycle instead of turning to motorized means of transport, thus, contributing to healthier natural ecosystems.[34] For individuals, studies have found that being in natural environments can reduce stress,[35] enhance quality of life[36] and restore cognitive attention.[37]

ACTIVITY-BASED LEARNING

#sleepymind

Sleep-time: Making the mind tired before sleep

#sleepymind

Today, expand your preparation for sleep by an additional ten minutes. Incorporate into your bed-time routine a period of time to engage in an activity with your child that will stimulate your child's mind. Let this activity take place long before your child starts to show signs of tiredness and ensure that only you know that you are both getting ready for bed. It is important that you find the right activity to suit your child while, where there are numerous children in the family, the activity may vary for each child. An activity that is the right fit is one your child is interested in doing, does not involve technology, can be done quietly, and involves full, undivided concentration. Recommended activities include 'color by number' pictures, jigsaws, crosswords, word-searches, writing stories or poems, drafts, cards or chess.

WHY AM I DOING THIS?

During your sleep, your brain is busy 'learning' all that it can from your daily experiences. It is also busy clearing out space for new experiences to be learned the following day. Ensuring that your child is cognitively stimulated during the day will help your child's brain know that it needs to sleep. In this activity, you are setting up a cue that the process of getting the mind and the body ready for sleep is approaching. Having a sleep routine is important in setting your child's biological sleep clock, which recognizes both physiological and environmental ques. It is important not to involve technology in these activities as artificial bright lights can interrupt the body's natural production of melatonin, a hormone released by the body when in darkness, that acts as a sleep signal to the body.[38]

FAMILY ATTACHMENT AND BONDING

#100 HAPPY DAYS 4 KIDS

#kidsday17

#colourfulmeal

Colourful meal

#colourfulmeal

Children and teenagers do not often associate food with art or creativity so today we will have a little work to do on changing this preconception. For breakfast, lunch and dinner, your child is asked to create the most colorful meal they can think of using foods appropriate to that particular meal. Fruits and vegetables will derive inspiration as they are the most colorful with lots of bright reds, sunny yellows and lush greens. It is perhaps a good idea to sit with your child the evening before in order to have their particulars in the house. You are encouraged to make this into a competition if you can, perhaps when a friend is over, and to have the children design their own meals. For example, they might want to put the toppings on their own pizzas to make interesting and unusual faces, objects or concepts. Needless to say, they can only win if they eat all of their creation! Upload your child's creations on to the #100happydays4kids website and have a wander through what other families around the world have eaten.

WHY AM I DOING THIS?

Transforming mealtime from just a mundane element of routine into a fun and creative experience allows children to view this time spent with family as something to look forward to. There are so many options for being creative with food that having a colorful meal is just an introduction. Family mealtimes have the potential for children to interact with their significant others in a way that can 'reinforce belonging and resiliency',[39] which leads to better overall psychological health. It is worth noting that language and social skills can be promoted through the experience of food in more ways than just sitting around a table. Meal-related activities such as writing the shopping list, packing snacks for school and picnics, and preparing vegetables are also valuable experiences to promote your child's development.[40]

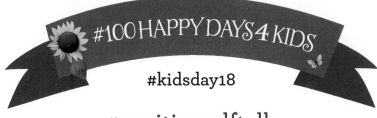

#kidsday18

#positiveselftalk

Positive self-talk

#positiveselftalk

WHAT DO I NEED TO DO?

Our thoughts become our words, our words become our action, our actions become our habits, and our habits become our destiny. It is logical to suggest that by changing our thoughts, we can change our destiny. This seems far-fetched but research does support that by simply changing our thought patterns, we can indeed change how we live our lives (see below). Negative thought processes are also often synonymous with anxiety, depression and other psychological disorders. The task today is to teach your child to replace these negative patterns with more helpful and useful thoughts. So, rather than focus on the negative aspects of life, your aim is to find the positive and highlight this to the child. Useful phrases may include, 'You got this; don't give up until you reach your goal', 'It's okay if we didn't win. We won the last time and we'll win again' or 'Volunteering makes me happy, despite the fact that no one thanked me today.'

WHY AM I DOING THIS?

Repeating self-statements such as 'I am beautiful' and 'I will have a great day today' are are extremely advantageous as they foster a positive mentality. Literature in the area of self-talk cites associations between self-talk and positive outcomes.[41] We are far too accustomed to engaging in negative self-talk as a direct result of the influence of mass media and a culture based fundamentally on unrealistic comparisons with ideal perfections. It is vital that we protect our children against this and work together toward empowering a more confident generation. Positive self-talk acts as a protector mechanism against psychological distress and difficulties by increasing independence, confidence and motivation, values which are necessary in any child's or adult's life. Studies have shown how self-talk is related to self-perception (what we think of ourselves) and self-esteem[42] (how we value ourselves); thus, by teaching our children how to improve these concepts, we can essentially change the quality of their lives.

FUNDAMENTAL PARENTING SKILL

#kidsday19

#tshirtoflove

T-shirt
of love

#tshirtoflove

Today, you are asked to get out the old white t-shirts you do not mind being scribbled on – one for you and one for mini-you. Place the t-shirts on a table with a panel of cardboard within so the marker does not bleed to the back. You and your child are asked to write five things you like about yourselves on the front, for example, 'I like my hair' or 'I like the way I am generous'. You are then asked to wear the t-shirts and write five things you like about the other person on the back of theirs. This is a great exercise for three or more in a family as you can guess who said what about you on your back. It might be worth framing this t-shirt, using it as a pajamas or wearing it during special family activities (if you used clothing markers) to keep the memory alive.

WHY AM I DOING THIS?

By each member of the family expressing what they appreciate and love about one another, you are encouraging a home environment which is caring and kind. This is one of the most beneficial outcomes you can have as a family, as it fosters independence, acceptance and celebration of individuals. This exercise of naming positive attributes is a family building exercise which allows each member to view one another from very different aspects. It might be surprising to hear what your child loves about you and for them to hear what you love the most about them. In a study conducted with poor minorities residing in a housing project in America, children frequently discussed how 'feeling loved' was special to them and how it helped them despite constant stressful triggers.[43] Understanding what a positive influence feeling loved has under these circumstances allows us to appreciate the power of love in our own home.

#kidsday20

#food4sleep

Sleep-time — A snack before bed

#food4sleep

Tonight, expand your preparation for sleep by an additional ten minutes. Ideally, after your 'tire the mind' activity, give your child a bed-time snack that will help to tire the body. Make sure your child chooses how much to eat or drink. Trust that their body knows how much it needs before bed. This snack does not need to become another meal you have to cook for your child, thus, adding pressure on to you. Instead, have something prepared earlier that you can just put on a plate for your child, such as a rice cake, home make biscuits, a fruit salad, or a banana and honey – you know best what snack your child will enjoy. The best type of food at this time of an evening is something that is wholesome to fill your child up, something that does not have much sugar in it, and something that your child will enjoy.

WHY AM I DOING THIS?

Certain foods and drinks help the body to produce the chemicals it needs for sleep. Evidence suggests that diet plays a contributory factor in how well one sleeps and that a lack of sleep is a contributor to obesity. Before bed, you want your child to have a snack that will help induce sleepiness. Carbohydrates cause tryptophan to be more available in the brain, which is an amino acid that is a precursor to the neurotransmitter, serotonin. This interacts with other brain areas to modulate circadian rhythm, sleep and waking.[44] Tryptophan is found in protein so cereal with milk, a cheese toasty, or the traditional warm milk and cookies are ideal snacks before bed. Bananas are also a useful bed-time snack to accompany a protein source as they contain carbohydrates, along with magnesium and potassium that contain natural muscle relaxation properties.

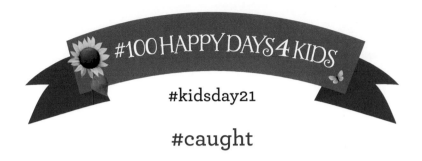

#caught

Caught!

#caught

Parents often pay immediate and full attention to children when they notice them acting unruly or exhibiting less favorable behavior. However, they often do not notice something wonderful their child just did. Your task is to take your child aside when you witness them showing good manners or being kind to a friend and praise them for their kindness, thoughtfulness and gentleness. Tell them that their excellent behavior and compassion for others makes you very proud to be their parent and you just wanted to let them know that. A private moment like this between parent and child is an invaluable experience as it promotes positive affect for both of you. Obviously, this praise will increase the likelihood of them continuing to show similar patterns of behavior into the future. Rather than leave this as a once-off, try to use this valuable parenting skill as a habit.

WHY AM I DOING THIS?

As well as encouraging children for displaying bigger and more obviously positive behaviors, such as cleaning their room for a treat, it is important that parents zone in on the more common-place and everyday behaviors which children also exhibit. Many children are accustomed to their parents calling them over after they have been unkind to a peer in the playground but have never experienced being called over after letting someone else have the swing. These small acts of kindness, thoughtfulness and gentleness are just as important as they display the character of your child.[45] Imagine how proud your child will be when they are praised for something that is just a part of who they are!

#kidsday22

#justbreathe

Just breathe and relax

#justbreathe

WHAT DO I NEED TO DO?

Look for as many opportunities as possible to pause what you are doing and just breathe. There are many times during any given day that we all just need to stop and center ourselves so that we can be our best in any given interaction. This is particularly important with our children because a parent's reaction means everything to a child. A negative reaction from a parent is not something that is just shrugged off; to a child, it manifests into the opinion they hold of themselves. Today, if you are feeling stressed, if your children are all demanding your attention at the one time, or if you are rushing but nobody seems to be able to go at your pace, try stopping momentarily and just breathing. Take a breath in through your nose at a slow pace and keep taking that breath in until you cannot fit any more air into your torso, then slowly release the breath back out. This breath will relax and center you back to being in a calmer position to manage the situation you are in.

WHY AM I DOING THIS?

The benefits of simply taking a breath are vast. In addition to evoking relaxation, taking a deep breath has been proven to affect the heart, the brain, and the immune system. Studies have shown that breathing exercises like the one in this task will immediately have a positive effect on blood pressure. Most importantly, engaging in these breathing exercises can be used as a method to train the body's reaction to stressful situations and dampen the production of harmful stress hormones. Physiologically, it has been shown that engaging in deep breathing exercises will stimulate a parasympathetic reaction, which calms one down. When your body is experiencing stress levels, it requires the vagus nerve to calm down, which is responsible for relaxation responses. When you take slow and deep breaths, you activate the vagus nerve and are thus dampening the body's stress response.[46]

FUNDAMENTAL PARENTING SKILL

#kidsday23

#scenicview

Scenic view

WHAT DO I NEED TO DO?

Today, you are asked to take yourself and your little one to a place of scenic beauty, whatever that means where you live. A field of animals, a river, a view of the city from a rooftop or a cathedral? Ask your child about what 'beauty' is to them and to point the beauty they can see from this spot. Sit with your child if you can and have a chat about the view, answering any questions they might have. Pull out the paper and crayons, and record this moment by drawing a picture. This can be a joint effort or two separate pictures for you both to compare. This task is important on two levels: firstly, it allows you to see the world through your child's eyes and to discuss how they see them and, secondly, it encourages you both to create a new memory on an otherwise uneventful morning or evening.

WHY AM I DOING THIS?

You may not have considered observing the world through your child's eyes but what would that perspective look like? There is no end to the amount of information we can learn from our children, such as how they feel around different people and how they make sense of complex concepts (like physics). Often, children make sense of the world in much more simplistic (and genius!) ways than adults ever could. The sight of a field of animals looks completely different to a child because of the new shapes, colors, dimensions, and behaviors that they observe in nature. Their height, intelligence and previous experience all make the conception of the experience very different from their parent and from other children. This is the very essence of perception: every person has their own completely unique view of the world and its workings. This form of insight can prove to be extremely beneficial[47] and can tailor future activities and relations for your family.

ACTIVITY-BASED LEARNING

#kidsday24

#familysleeptime

Sleep-time: Make it family time

#familysleeptime

Tonight, expand upon your preparation for sleep-time by another additional ten minutes and incorporate into your bed-time preparations some opportunity for family time. It is certainly not always possible to have the whole family home before the first child's bed-time; however, plan to make this happen for today. There is plenty of time during preparation for bed to simply be as a family, with no agenda, no phones, no online chatting, no dinner, and no activity whatsoever, except just appreciating being at home together as a family. This does not have to be a forced activity but rather is something that should just happen after everyone has finished their night-time snack – everyone is simply there together. Your role now is to lead your family to being mindful of this present state, which can be done by simply commenting on how lovely it is for everyone to just be together. Keep the conversation in the here and now; help your family to appreciate the moment they are in. Draw attention to a scent, a sight, a sound, a touch, or a taste that everyone can attend to at that present moment. For example, 'There is a beautiful smell off that candle on the table', 'Isn't that picture of us on the wall lovely?', 'The sound of laughter in the room is so great to hear', 'My dressing gown feels so soft' or 'I can still taste the yummy hot milk that we had'.

WHY AM I DOING THIS?

In this task, you are helping your child connect with the world they are presently in before they embark on the journey that processes and enables the learning of all that was perceived during the day. This is the journey of sleep. By following the 'how to' of the task today, you are engaging in a mindfulness practice with your child by helping them to bring their awareness fully onto the moment they are presently in and allowing them to enjoy feelings of security and by tuning into the family that surrounds them. As a child prepares to embark on their journey of sleep each night, thoughts and feelings of anxiety from the day gone by are often raised and the practice of this task will help bring some calm. Engaging in mindfulness practice has been shown to be useful in the promotion of improved sleep, with studies showing that mindfulness practice frequency is positively correlated with increased sleep duration.[48]

#kidsday25

#freeculture

Visit a free museum/ heritage center

#freeculture

WHAT DO I NEED TO DO?

Let's inject some culture into these happy days! Today, you are asked to take your child to a free museum and spend quality time there talking about what life is like for other people and how this is represented in the different pieces. Of course, there is no rule that states you cannot bring him/her to a museum you love which you can pay into – this is perfect as it is something that you are passionate about and this excitement tends to be contagious. If you need any extra help, you can ask a worker there to tell some stories about the different pieces on show. It is important for children to be aware of how different life is for children and adults all around the world, as it broadens their perspective and horizon. For the most pleasurable experience, make a day out of it and take the train into the city for a coffee and milkshake before a trip to the museum or heritage center.

WHY AM I DOING THIS?

Museum and heritage centers are social areas where children investigate historical or novel items and concepts which they make sense of using their own knowledge, background, customs and beliefs. A recent study[49] has found how children responded to four different museums (natural and social history, art gallery, science centre, and art/social history) in different unique ways because of their own previous understanding, curiosity, and socio-cultural circumstances. As a result, every single child's memory or impact from the visits was completely different. It is important for parents to understand that their child will have their very own 'fingerprint' reaction to different museum or heritage exhibits, cognitively, aesthetically, motivationally, and collaboratively. Therefore, the more parents introduce their children to the differing types of exhibits and heritage opportunities in their communities, the more exposure the child will have to new internal experiences that are unique to them. These unique experiences have a huge impact on the child's cognitive, creative and social ability.

Take some time today to pause and reflect on your happiness levels over the last 26 days of your challenge

#pause2reflect

WHAT DO I NEED TO DO?

Focus on how much happier you are feeling now compared to twenty-five days ago.

DOCUMENT & SHARE

Why not document your experience on **www.100happydays4kids.com** where you can share your experience with others and see how people from around the world are benefiting from engaging in this challenge?

Do not forget to share your journey of happiness with your friends too!

FUNDAMENTAL PARENTING SKILL

#kidsday27

#run4fun

Run 4 fun!

#run4fun

WHAT DO I NEED TO DO?

Run, run, run – just for fun! All you need is your child, an open space, and the motivation to run. This can be done anywhere – a park, a field, a meadow, a beach, a forest, a garden… literally anywhere! You do not need lots of time, toys or a special place – you just need your willingness and a good attitude. Children do not need to be running after or for anything. Simply running around together embracing the freedom to do so is enough for a child. This is an experience – running aimlessly, at your own pace, slowing and pausing when you please, laughing and breathing at your ease, feeling the wind and the movement fresh upon your face.

WHY AM I DOING THIS?

Free running is of huge physical and emotional benefit to your child. When running freely, you are connecting with your body, physically controlling it and tuning into our bodies to identify what it needs at any given time. You are present in the moment with your body as you do not have any other aim, such as in football when you are focused on the ball rather than on the running itself. When engaged in this type of fast-paced activity, your body is releasing feel good hormones known as endocannabinoids. A huge body of research exists to support the fact that running will enhance your emotional wellbeing. Just thirty minutes of running during the week for three weeks boosts sleep quality, mood and concentration during the day.[50]

ACTIVITY-BASED LEARNING

#100 HAPPY DAYS 4 KIDS

#kidsday28

#sensorysleep

Sleep-time: Share in a sensory experience with your child

#sensorysleep

WHAT DO I NEED TO DO?

As before, expand your preparation for sleep-time by an additional ten minutes tonight. Incorporate into your bed-time preparations time to share a sensory experience with your child. This experience can be anything you wish as long as it involves safe touch and is something that your child enjoys. You must follow your child's comfort levels on this one. If your child becomes ticklish, giggly, agitated, or in any way uncomfortable, simply stop what you are doing and explain that you are stopping because you noticed that he or she was starting to look, for instance, uncomfortable. There are many possibilities for this activity, including a baby massage, a clap-hands game, writing a message, drawing a shape with your finger on the palm of your child's hand, stroking your child's arm, giving your child a hand or foot massage and painting your child's finger- or toe-nails.

WHY AM I DOING THIS?

The benefits of skin-to-skin contact between a mother and her newborn have been well documented. Through the sensory stimulation created by touch, warmth and odor, this contact releases maternal oxytocin which results in decreased maternal anxiety, increased calmness, and enhanced parenting behaviors.[51] With benefits like this, the question is not why do we engage in skin-to-skin contact, but rather why do we stop? This is particularly true when research shows that touch is essential for child development and mental health. Studies have demonstrated a positive relationship between tactile stimulation and physical growth, brain development, and social-emotional development.[52] To ensure safe touch practices, the tactile experience will be in response to the needs of the child only. Permission will be asked first regardless of how young the child is. For example, before a baby massage, open your hands and say 'Mammy is going to give you a massage now. Is that okay?' and the touch will stop if the child shows any indications of discomfort. The type of tactile stimulation provided should be appropriate for the age and developmental stage of the child.

#doagooddeed

Today, my child and I will do a good deed together

#doagooddeed

Today, you are asked to guide your child through what may be the first random act of kindness. It is vital that the child can really feel as though they are part of the process, if not leading the act. For example, suggested activities include baking scones for a busy friend, visiting an elderly neighbor, or putting something nice in the mailbox for the postman. However, the child might have their very own idea of how to complete this exercise. Even just the experience of parent-child idea-sharing will increase relationship quality and mutual regard. A key component of parenting is 'modelling' or vicarious learning, whereby children watch their parents and mimic their actions, words and feelings. This is how children learn a surprising amount of information, which we often take for granted. Have you ever thought how children can form grammatically-correct sentences before they even start school? It is beneficial for children to witness their parents being kind to others, with no selfish benefits, as it encourages altruism: the practice of unselfish concern for the well-being of others.

WHY AM I DOING THIS?

Altruism is a naturally developing trait in all children as research has shown that babies help unfamiliar people without indication, advice or help from another person[53,54] and attempt to respond to the emotional needs of others, showing empathy for those in distress.[55] Parental example-setting is such an important factor in the development of children's altruistic abilities, in that high levels of empathy are associated with altruistic behavior in children.[56]

Make a card

#makeacard

WHAT DO I NEED TO DO?

There is so much sentimentality behind giving someone a card. You are expressing to the receiver that you want them to have a good time on their birthday, that you wish for their family to have a wonderful new year or that you are thinking of them and that they are not alone. Today you are asked to help create and design a card with your child for anyone in their life that they want. It could be a birthday card for an uncle, a 'Get Well Soon' card for someone who is sick, or an invitation to a tea-party at your house. Adding this personal touch is something that makes their creation unique and makes the message it contains so much more special.

WHY AM I DOING THIS?

There are some behaviors that come more naturally to children than to adults and one of those is giving. Children are keenly interested in wanting to give gifts to others and research has shown that their moral reasoning is a key predictor of this type of behavior.[57] This means that even young children are able to think about the gift of giving and rationalize why it is an activity they choose to do. If all children have this almost identical opinion and so young, it may suggest that giving is engrained into our DNA. Giving is one of the main behaviors which distinguish us from other species,[58] which is further evidence that it may be an integral component of our make-up. Whatever the case, it is an extremely important trait that must be fostered and enhanced in children as it helps cooperation in social relationships and interactions.[59]

FUNDAMENTAL PARENTING SKILL

#messyplay

Today is for messy play – your way!

#messyplay

WHAT DO I NEED TO DO?

Basically – get messy! You can do this in whatever way you want. You may decide to do one activity that involves all of your family or you may decide to provide different messy play opportunities for each of your children. You need to look at your own comfort levels before deciding where to engage in messy play to make sure you will show your child all the way through the activity that they are free to be as messy as they please. You will show this best by joining in freely and, when you are fully immersed in the activity, you will be less inclined to start limiting mess as you go. Your activity can be a water fight, a mud bath, body paint, natural make-up, free-style baking, fixing a car, or anything else you can think of. It just needs to be messy!

WHY AM I DOING THIS?

Messy play is a fundamental part of the creative process through which children learn and develop.[60] The process involved in messy play can be equated with Piaget's concept of cognitive disequilibrium, whereby one's thinking has to be altered for the incorporation of newly acquired information.[61] Thus, it is through new experiences that a child's interpretation of the world is developed. The benefits of messy play are that it is always a new experience, all the materials are changeable and interchangeable, a child's manipulation of the materials will lead to endless possibilities, and the only limit on the play is that of the child's imagination, which will develop and expand through their experiences of messy play. For children of all ages, it is good for them to have control over some process and messy play provides that perfect opportunity.

ACTIVITY-BASED LEARNING

#relax4sleep

Sleep-time: Relax, imagine and love

#relax4sleep

Tonight you are adding the last step into your sleep routine so, again, expand your preparation for sleep time by an additional ten minutes. Then, following from the sensory experience with your child, add a relaxation period. This can be particularly useful when dividing your time between a number of children in different rooms, and the relaxation stage can come before or after the sensory experience depending on how many children you have. The main aim of the relaxation period is to allow your child to simply be, to let their mind settle down after the day and to prepare itself for all the processing of the day that takes place whilst the child is sleeping. To help your child relax, you can light a candle, turn on a lava lamp or a night-light, or place some lavender by the bed. Once the child has had a few minutes 'down-time', introduce the bed-time story. Read the story quietly and slowly to the child while they are in their bed, allowing them to watch the book as you read. Some children will want to read their own stories at this time, and other children will want to read alone without you in the room – follow your child's lead on this. One thing that remains the same for all children of all ages (and many adults too!) is the benefit of hearing the words 'I love you' last thing before going to sleep. As such, end your child's day with these words, regardless of their age.

WHY AM I DOING THIS?

Regardless of how your day was with your child, you wipe the slate clean with the three words 'I love you' before they go to sleep. Many children hear anxiety-inducing words last thing before they go to sleep such as 'Go to sleep now'. This will lead to the child trying to force sleep and, thus, waking up the mind again. You are trying to calm your child as much as possible so that they naturally drift into a sleep when their mind is ready to do so. A story can help at this time as it detaches the child from their thoughts and channels the mind to focus on the story, thus, helping the child to be present in the moment they are in. Reading aloud to children when in a place of calm like created in the final version of the Sleep-time sequences can further reduce a child's cortisol levels, which directly lower stress levels. Studies have found a clear neurological difference between children who are read to regularly and children who are not.[62]

Bake 'n' give

#bakengive

Today, you are asked to grab some flour, flick the oven on and get creative. There are no set rules about what you should bake but something which can be sliced up is a good idea. Have in mind a person, group of people or organization you want to give this batch to and consider with your child what they might like (note: dietary requirements). Allow your child as much freedom as possible about the creative aspect of the baking – the color of the icing, the type of sweets to put in the cookies or the flavor of the ice-cream. Is there a neighbor who rarely gets visitors or a group of people working hard for a good cause? Really make an effort to have your child be a part of the decision-making process so they feel all the benefits of giving in the community: planning, rationalizing, and being proactive. Allow today to be messy, child-centered and fun by creating characters (Le Chef Mom-mee) or adding music.

WHY AM I DOING THIS?

This type of learning whereby the child actively gets involved with their caregiver during the activity is called 'guided participation',[63] and is based on a model of learning that is likened to an apprenticeship. As such, they are placed in an actual kitchen with real appliances and a master to guide, give advice and oversee all of their work. In this kitchen, your child will learn through receiving clear instructions as well as through real participation. Importantly, Le Chef Mom-mee also learns new creative techniques and ideas from the equally important sous-chef. Facilitating the child's learning of a new skill and creation of a new product allows them to feel increased self-esteem, while allowing the child to make decisions about who to give the cookies to also allows them to feel mature and trusted. This heightened self-esteem and independence are two of the most important traits of the learning child,[64] and are fundamental contributory factors towards the active learning of new skills.

INDEPENDENCE BUILDING

#kidsday34

#chooseyourreaction

Choose your reaction

#chooseyourreaction

Today, you are asked to teach your child a new lesson, which may also be a new lesson for you. When less than perfect things happen to us, we automatically think about resorting to the old reliables of distress, anger or upset. However, did you know that we can actually choose how we want to react? So, ask your child to imagine a situation such as when their friend asks them to come to party. Next, ask them to imagine all the different ways they could react. This can be a game where you are the friend asking them and they have to act out how they would react. They might react in a happy, angry, sad or silly way? They might feel embarrassed, excited or blessed. Try to think of as many ways as you can to show your child how there is not ONE way of reacting; they can choose to react in healthier ways.

WHY AM I DOING THIS?

Emotional regulation refers to one's ability to successfully manage emotions to secure effective social functioning.[65] When a child is able to functionally manage their emotions such that there is no negative effect on others around then, they are regarded as being able to regulate their emotions effectively. However, when their reactions have detrimental effects on those around them, it is referred to as 'emotional dysregulation'. Poor regulation of anger and exuberance is associated with externalizing problems in children, such as behavioral difficulties, while good regulation is associated with prosocial behaviors, such as being a good team-member.[66] These researchers also found that poor fear regulation is associated with internalizing problems, namely difficulties with social anxiety. Teaching a child all of the different ways they can react is effective as it allows them to regulate their emotions and explore different responses. Their different responses will attract different reactions from their peers also, which can teach the child what are the most accepted and beneficial reactions for them to choose.

#sensoryplay

Today is for sensory play – do it your way!

#sensoryplay

WHAT DO I NEED TO DO?

Today, you will facilitate your child's engagement in sensory play. If possible, doing this outdoors will add to the sensory experience as the child will benefit from the natural smells of the environment, the feeling of the wind or rain on their skin, and from hearing the surrounding sounds. Your sensory activity can be created using what is naturally available to you. Create an imaginary outdoor kitchen using mud, water, stones, sticks, and leaves. Children of all ages can benefit from this task. Even babies direct themselves towards sensory play at all given opportunities; however, this natural gravitation decreases as children get older. A sensory play experience exists for all ages – sitting on the grass, making a daisy-chain, creating a flower arrangement, building a hut, building a camping area, or freestyle painting.

WHY AM I DOING THIS?

Sensory play is very important for every child, as we are able to learn through all of our senses. If we are only given the opportunity to learn through one or two of our senses, we are missing out on other key learning opportunities. This applies to everyone - from babies right through to adults. Think about how much can be learned from an interactive live cooking demonstration compared to reading a recipe. Through sensory play, children enhance their cognitive development, social skills, sense of self, physical skills, emotional development, and communication skills. Offering children a comfortable and accommodating environment for sensory play will make the child feel at ease and, thus, able them to follow their instincts and interests.[67]

ACTIVITY-BASED LEARNING

#100 HAPPY DAYS 4 KIDS

#kidsday36

#sharingiscaring

Share something you have never shared before

#sharingiscaring

WHAT DO I NEED TO DO?

You are back on 'friends' territory today as this task involves telling your child something you have never told him/her before. They are asked to also share something they have never shared with you before too. This can be as light-hearted, humorous or deep as you both want. It really does not matter what this new knowledge is, big or small; the aim is for you both to learn something new about one another, for example, 'I sing in the shower' or 'I go for coffee with Lisa while waiting for your dance class to finish'. The task does not end with this. You are then asked to respect your child's new knowledge, and to not to use it against them or make fun of their choice in any way. In essence, this means to be 'non-judgemental'. The aim today is to establish and build upon trust between yourself and your child.

WHY AM I DOING THIS?

The task today is designed to foster enhanced communication skills between you and your child in a simple way, which is accessible to all. Accepting what your child says without reaction will allow them to see that they can share anything with you and not be anxious about how you will react. Harboring mistakes and problems is detrimental to one's health and leads to catastrophizing, obsessive thoughts and chronic anxiety. Communication is a deliberate interaction between two or more people which does not only convey information over and back, but also defines the relationship between the two.[68] When talking to someone is easy or fun, we think of that person in a positive way; however, when attempts at communication are difficult and conflict regularly arises, we tend to think of that person in a less positive light. Take today to think about how you can become a more receptive and calm listener to your child.

Today, I will hand over the meal planning duties to my child

#mealplanner

WHAT DO I NEED TO DO?

You will be handing meal planning control over to your child today. However, they will need your help to fully execute this task. Start by helping your child to choose a meal that will suit all of your family's needs. Next, help your child choose the ingredients that are needed. You may have some at home already so child can physically gather them up and others may need to be bought. If you are buying the ingredients for the meal, let the child guide the list-making process and the shopping experience. A picture shopping list can be useful to help younger children be involved in the shopping, a template of which can be found in the members' section of www.100happydays4kids.com. Once all the ingredients are in place, encourage your child to think about how you cook the meal and, where possible, follow their guidance on this.

WHY AM I DOING THIS?

Under the United Nations Convention of the Rights of the Child (UNCROC), there are two articles that provide for the rights of the child in making decisions. Article 12 of UNCROC requires that children have the right to express their opinions freely and to have that opinion considered in decisions that affect them. Article 13 recognizes the right of children to seek, receive and provide information and ideas of all kinds.[69] What better place to start helping your child exercise these rights than with their own food! Today, you are engaging with what is known as 'The Family Food Decision-Making Cycle', which provides the foundation for understanding family food decision-making. Stages in the family food decision-making cycle are: (1) determining issues associated with a food event that requires considering alternatives outside the usual routines and established food policies; (2) identifying and assessing perceived practically available alternatives to meet family goals; (3) evaluating and choosing among the alternatives; and (4) implementing the chosen alternative.[70]

INDEPENDENCE BUILDING

Today, I will express unconditional love even when the child feels as though they failed

#unconditionallove

WHAT DO I NEED TO DO?

This activity was designed for you to show your child complete acceptance and positive regard when they feel as though they did not accomplish what they sought to do. Positive expressions during times like these show the child that you love them, not for their successes, but for being THEM; that they do not need to earn your love; and that making you proud is not necessary. The child will understand that just being themselves deserves the most natural and powerful of all emotions: a parent's love for their child. This exercise need not be used for obvious negative events, such as your child feeling disappointed that they come last in a race. While this is the perfect opportunity to shower them with unconditional love, it might not happen very often. This practice can be done when the child is sad that they have colored outside the lines, when they cannot make the perfect mold with the play-dough, or when they cannot tie their shoe-laces without some help. Just take some time to communicate to them that they are special, loved and valued no matter what.

WHY AM I DOING THIS?

This type of acceptance promotes a healthy view of success, as it suggests that personal achievements are not the only way to gain parental approval, although they do feel good for the child. The satisfying feeling of accomplishment is something that all children should enjoy but the worry of disappointing parents after 'failure' is not. Research has shown that a style of parenting that promotes listening to the child and encouraging independence, combined with high levels of parental warmth and love, contribute to a sense of security in children.[71] This type of parent-child relationship leads to a more holistic development of emotional regulation.

FUNDAMENTAL PARENTING SKILL

#kidsday39

#freeplay

Free play

#freeplay

WHAT DO I NEED TO DO?

Today, just let them play! For this, you simply need to set the scene and watch them go. This can be done anywhere and by any means. The important thing is that they are in a place that does not confine them to rules. If they want to be messy, they can. If they want to use toys, they can. If they want to pretend, they can. If they want to climb, they can. You are allowing each child to play in accordance with the limits that they set only for themselves. This activity must come from each child's own imagination; all you have to do is allow them to tap into their innate creativity, permit them to be themselves and let them shape their own boundaries and rules. A simple line such as 'Today you can play in your own way' will adequately inform the child of the concept of the day.

WHY AM I DOING THIS?

Despite the benefits derived from play for both children and parents, a report by the American Academy of Paediatrics[72] found that time for free-play has been markedly reduced for some children. This report addressed a variety of factors that have reduced play, including a hurried lifestyle, changes in family structure, and increased attention to academics. Free-play has been shown to allow children to use their creativity while developing their imagination, dexterity, and physical, cognitive, and emotional strength.[73] When play is allowed to be free and child-driven, children practice decision-making skills, move at their own pace, discover their own areas of interest, and ultimately engage fully in the passions they wish to pursue.[74] Additionally, it is suggested that encouraging unstructured play may be an exceptional way to increase physical activity levels in children.[75]

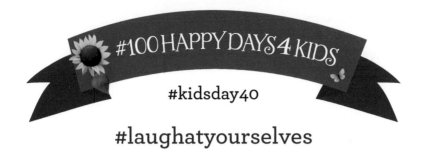

#laughatyourselves

Laugh at yourselves

#laughatyourselves

Life should not be taken too seriously and children in particular should not feel the pressures of perfection or failure. Your task today is to teach your child to laugh at themselves, instead of sulking or being upset. Choose a time when you notice your child is feeling embarrassed or confused over a situation and explain to them that sometimes it is really healthy to look back on a situation and just laugh about it. Show them how there are some times in life that need to be taken seriously, but this was not one and that laughing about it is a good way to let it go. Encouraging your child to laugh at him/herself is a valuable way to spend thirty minutes but remember to lead by example too. Always praise your child any time you notice them overcoming a situation by utilizing their sense of humor.

WHY AM I DOING THIS?

Humor is often regarded as a characteristic that is pleasurable but not necessarily an important trait to have. Few people consider humor to be a skill or strength that can be utilized to improve situations. However, there is much more to having a good sense of humor than simply making silly jokes. Research has shown that using humor leads to friends being able to 'laugh things off' rather than allowing it to cause conflict between members.[76] This diffusion of tension does not come naturally to everyone and some children need to be taught how to not take things too seriously. Feelings of embarrassment, annoyance or regret can often be turned around when looked at through a different lens and life lessons can be learned much easier with a sprinkling of humor. You would be amazed what you could overcome by simply laughing about it!

#irespectyouropinion

I respect your opinion

#irespectyouropinion

WHAT DO I NEED TO DO?

There are lots of times when families have debates and arguments about both trivial and bigger issues. These can usually be sorted out with some discussion after both parties have calmed down. However, oftentimes there does not seem to be any middle ground, making conflict resolution a little further from sight. This is an unfortunate part of life that all children need to be taught. One essential skill for parents and children to learn is that, although you may often completely disagree with one another's opinion, you should respect that they have an opinion. As such, your task today is to have a chat with your child about how opinions are formed, that others will always have different opinions and that this is what creates so much diversity in the world. Expressing a different opinion is not always easy but we are all entitled to express our feelings. Respecting others' and having your opinion respected allows for a clearer evaluation and often a calmer debate and compromise.

WHY AM I DOING THIS?

Respecting others' opinions is considered to be a prosocial coping skill because there will be numerous times in your child's life when they will be faced with conflict, a mutually agreeable resolution will not be possible and s/he will have to accept that. It is best for the child if they can learn this lesson in the safety and comfort of their family and home environment, which is non-threatening and accepting. Learning these prosocial skills at home in this support social context prepares the child to regulate their own emotions when they are at school or college and socializing with a myriad of different people. Complex social difficulties arise all the time when a variety of opinions, values and backgrounds are constantly being discussed and debated. Learning this skill early in your child's life will contribute to a much easier emotional path and will lead to fewer socio-emotional and behavioral difficulties.[77]

INDEPENDENCE BUILDING

#sitnlearn

Sit 'n' learn

#sitnlearn

WHAT DO I NEED TO DO?

Today is a day for Mammy/Daddy to do some learning themselves. The task is quite simple but will hopefully result in you understanding a little bit more about this little person in your life. When your child is engaging in society (on a play-date or in the playground), just sit and observe them interacting with others, without your input, support or judgment. Watch how s/he socializes with others, tackles the monkey-bars and plays with the sand. How does your child view and interact with other children? How does your child play with the toys, run in the wind or laugh on the swing? How is your child developing as an individual person? Take some time to think about how your child has changed since s/he came into your life. Spend these few moments appreciating who this little person is, who they are becoming and what makes them smile.

WHY AM I DOING THIS?

By practicing the art of observation, you are actively engaging in a key component of 'mindful' parenting. This type of parenting is tapping into 'the awareness that emerges through paying attention, on purpose, in the present moment, and nonjudgmentally to the unfolding of experience moment by moment'.[78] This means that you are not focusing on what happened yesterday, what will happen tomorrow or what is happening on the other side of the wall. You are intently focusing on your little person and noticing their personalities, social interactions and your feelings. Logging these observations (or revelations) on paper or in digital formal is like keeping these musings safe in a time-capsule that can be revisited later in their lives. This form of parental reflection ensures that the fleeting childhood of this little person is slowed down a little, enough to pay attention to the small things.

FUNDAMENTAL PARENTING SKILL

#fourseasonssummer

Four seasons - Summer

#fourseasonssummer

WHAT DO I NEED TO DO?

Today, we will share Vivaldi's Four Seasons with our child again to promote the connections between emotions, music and art. Specifically, we will be focusing on the second movement of Summer (Adagio). Children often do not have the language to communicate emotions and these words are not always needed or desired. Even as adults, it is not always necessary to discuss our state of mind, thoughts and emotions with others; it is often favorable instead to channel these through art, dance or crafts. Please reflect on how the Spring movement went for you and your child. Is there anything you would like to add or change? Different textures (sand, leaves) or different tools (crayon, markers)? Did your child enjoy talking to you about what they painted? Use this reflection to inform the quality time you spend with your child today. Like the last time, explain that this music represents a time of the year and ask them to create a masterpiece reflecting what they see in their imagination.

WHY AM I DOING THIS?

The health benefits of relaxing music are widely documented in the literature as having powerful effects on social, emotional and mental functioning, as well as one's mood.[79] The power of music is so extensive, it has been shown to produce significant positive effects on patients with health problems.[80,81,82] Despite the fact that your child may not explicitly state that they enjoy Bach, this music was recommended for its relaxing qualities. Personal preferences do not seem to have much effect on the relaxation response of individuals listening to soothing music.[83] Producing a picture of what they envisage during this calm time allows the child to capture what feeling relaxed looks like and can serve as a reminder and prompt if posted on their wall.

#kidsday44

#randomcelebration

Random celebration

#randomcelebration

WHAT DO I NEED TO DO?

Why do we always wait for something to come along to have a celebration? We should never take for granted that we are here, that we have this moment, and that this moment is real and precious. It is often only when unpleasant circumstances occur in our lives that we take the time to appreciate how perfect and amazing our life was. As parents, it is important to pass on the knowledge that there is so much happiness in every moment when you are together as a family. As such, your task today is to surprise your family with a random celebration. You can call it something like like 'We are Alive', 'Just Because…' or 'Why Not?' and you are asked to pull out the party hats, slice up the chocolate cake and turn up the music. Do not wait until tomorrow for the opportunity to celebrate how amazing your little family is.

WHY AM I DOING THIS?

More often than not, we tend to look around to circumstances in which we find ourselves in to decide what we need to be doing or feeling. If you really think about it, we usually find ourselves only eating turkey on Christmas day or only writing a kind sentiment for friends on their birthday. Similarly, when we feel emotions, we tend to feel them because an event or situation occurred and our emotions were reactions to these. There is no need to allow your circumstances to affect your emotions or behavior – they belong to you. Focusing on what is positive in your life, celebrating it and feeling grateful for your child, family, health, home and whole life is vital for remaining in the moment. This kind of happiness is much more gratifying than any material item acquired and being fully mindful of what is good in your life has the potential to provide freedom from the attempt to gain pleasure from other sources that are ultimately short-lived and dissatisfying.[84]

#growthegood

Today, I will give my child the opportunity to discover where their food comes from by helping them to grow their favorite fruit or vegetable

#growthegood

WHAT DO I NEED TO DO?

Explore with your child the origin of their favorite fruit and vegetables. You can do this by creating a scrapbook with pictures or printouts of the journey that takes place from being a seed to becoming an edible food. Once your child has a conceptual idea of the journey of a seed, you can then start deciding on what the most suitable food for you to grow is, taking into consideration your space, climate, the time it takes, and the level of care required. You then embark on your own journey with your specially selected seeds by planting them, taking care of them, watching them grow, and then eventually enjoying the benefits of eating them. Ensure that your children take the lead on all involved with this task – your role is simply to facilitate and support them when needed.

WHY AM I DOING THIS?

In addition to the endless benefits of getting outside with your child and engaging in a natural material activity, this particular task has a variety of extra benefits for your child's well-being. You want to show your child that they have the ability to become self-sufficient, an important part of which is having the means to provide food for yourself. Children who grow their own food have been found, by a large number of studies, to be more likely to eat fruits and vegetables and to show higher levels of knowledge about nutrition.[85] This activity can potentially impact upon lifelong influences as studies show that children who grow their own food were more likely to continue healthy eating habits throughout their lives. Research has also shown that people who reported picking vegetables, taking care of plants, or living next to a garden in childhood were more likely to continue gardening and to form lasting positive relationships with gardens and trees into adulthood.

Direct a random act of kindness to your nearest and dearest – your child

#randomactofkindness

WHAT DO I NEED TO DO?

Parents are often so engrossed in positively reinforcing good behaviors, manners and school-work that it is easy to forget how to just randomly do something nice for your child. This random act will be something that your child has not earned, asked for or expected. Children often think about bringing gifts home for their parents when out and about. There is no nicer feeling than receiving a squished flower-head from a smiling child after they return from a trip to the park. So, today, return the favor and bring about that same feeling in your child. You can decide on the most fitting random act of kindness suited to your child, from picking them a flower on your way home from work to drawing them a picture, writing them a note, giving them a lipstick kiss on paper or carrying their school bag for them. The only rule is that it must demonstrate kindness randomly.

WHY AM I DOING THIS?

This simple act of giving fosters care and cooperation in social interactions. Studies show that we feel happier when we perform acts of kindness, regardless of who is at the receiving end. What about making our children happier? Research has found that giving behaviors spread so, by having your child on the receiving end of your random act of kindness, you will most likely see them pay it forward.[86] This, in turn, can result in your child feeling increased levels of happiness and well-being, as well as enjoying an improvement in the quality of their friendships.[87]

Dress up for role-play

#roleplay

WHAT DO I NEED TO DO?

Today, you simply dress up and have fun! Children naturally gravitate towards dressing up and playing out roles such as princesses, superheroes, rescue service people and health-care workers. Adults do not tend to do this so much, which is a shame as it provides the perfect opportunity to detach from yourself, for a period of time. So, today, take some time to play dress-up with your children, regardless of their age. Be as creative as you can, designing a costume that will allow you play any role you wish. Use anything you can find – sheets, blankets, clothes, shoes, jackets, masks, hair pieces, face paint, make-up and jewelry. The real fun is in the process – working together and finding as many ways as possible to be something or someone different. When doing this, the traditional roles of 'parent' and 'child' are left behind and you become the role that you want to play, as do they.

WHY AM I DOING THIS?

Dress-up play is a very beneficial activity for children of all ages as it allows the child to step outside of their regular role and into the role of another. It is by doing this that a child learns to understand other roles as distinct from their own. This is important play to facilitate as it allows for a child's psychological growth and gives them an opportunity to practice ways of forming an understanding of others, of relationships, and of the world in which they live. Children will learn about gender roles through dressing up and about domestic roles by taking on the pretend role of different family members. Children also use role-play to navigate their way through life's social rules. By being a part of this play with your child, you are being a part of a huge phase of your child's development of social understanding.[88]

ACTIVITY-BASED LEARNING

Tales of babyhood

#talesofbabyhood

WHAT DO I NEED TO DO?

Today, we are getting nostalgic! If you have old baby photos of yourself, pull them out and compare them to photos of your child. Talk to your child about how being a child when you were young was different and ask for their opinions. Ask them what being a child now is like (for example, using Skype, watching TV from around the world and going on a plane). Talk to your child about what they would be like if they were a Mammy/Daddy like you. This simple exercise could really take longer than the recommended fifteen minutes, and you are encouraged to enjoy engaging with your child on this new level. You may find that younger children will be intrigued by the fact that their parent was once a child too and older children will be fascinated by how you spent your childhood without social media.

WHY AM I DOING THIS?

In this time of busy families who are bombarded by play-dates, educational challenges and a constant flow of information through digital media, it is no surprise that sharing simple yet important family moments are often the last things we have time to do. This book has been designed to guide you through how to facilitate these tasks in your family in short bouts of time, which have a great deal of benefits for your family. If you do not have a large quantity of spare time to spend with your children, you need to ensure it is quality time! Sharing your childhood with your child allows them to relate to you on a different level, as they may not have considered that you were once just like them. Telling family stories allows children to understand and celebrate aspects of their shared situations.[89]

#timeapart

Time apart

#timeapart

WHAT DO I NEED TO DO?

You may be surprised that this task is included; however, it is vital for all relationships that you spend some time apart. The main aim is to spend enjoyable time apart with a pre-determined time of when you will both be coming home. Kids can be asked how they would like to spend a day (at a friend's house, camp or activity center) and you are required to have a soothing massage, play a round of competitive golf or enjoy a lavish lunch-date with a group of friends. Frequent check-ins with one another are allowed during the day but the main aim is to consider what you, as a person, and what your child, as an individual, enjoy doing without fitting into a role of being father and daughter, for example. This self-care is vital for healthy personal development and for a positive outlook about your own life separate to being Mom or Dad.

WHY AM I DOING THIS?

Everything in moderation, as the saying goes. While being a parent or being part of a family cannot really be done in moderation, it is still necessary to take breaks from the very routine ordinariness of daily life. Just because you are a parent does not mean that you should not participate in other activities or socialize with other people. Equally, your child needs to be able to foster other social relationships outside of the family in a supportive environment but without your guidance. You can rest assured that, while you are taking a wee break for yourself, you are doing this for the benefit of your family! Allowing your child to experience social relationships separate from their family allows them to develop their own sense of identity and helps foster emotional independence.[90] These are important tools for your child who is developing into a strong and resilient person.

#pause2reflect

Take some time today to pause and reflect on your children's happiness levels now that you have reached the half-way point of your challenge

#pause2reflect

WHAT DO I NEED TO DO?

Focus on how much happier your children are feeling now compared to fifty days ago.

DOCUMENT & SHARE

Why not document your experience on **www.100happydays4kids.com** where you can share your experience with others and see how people from around the world are benefiting from engaging in this challenge?

Do not forget to share your journey of happiness with your friends too!

#puppeteering

Puppeteering

#puppeteering

WHAT DO I NEED TO DO?

Time to raid the odd socks drawer! Today, you are asked to play puppets with your child where they pretend to be you and you pretend to be him/her – role reversal. It is important today for your child to choose the sock or puppet which they feel represents you, while you will also choose a sock or puppet to represent your child. A short game of fifteen or twenty minutes is sufficient for you both to get into character and do a role-play of a few scenarios. You will learn what you are like in your child's eyes and how they perceive you, for example, important, rule-setting, fun or silly. It might be nice to spend a few minutes documenting how you feel afterwards and if there are any changes you would like to make to your parenting style.

WHY AM I DOING THIS?

Role-play is a technique children use in order to interact with their world and make sense of its structures, which are complex to the young, growing and curious brain.[91] Research has shown that children as young as two- to three-years of age have the ability to understand and know about other roles so well that they can change their behavior accordingly.[92] This means that we can use role-play as an effective method of learning more about what children understand and know about their parents' roles. This information can then be used to further educate the child about what other roles parents have (support) and what roles they do not have (disallowing adventure). As such, role-play can be used as a mirror for you to have a look at your parenting from your child's perspective.

ACTIVITY-BASED LEARNING

#kidsday52

#familygame

A game for all the family

#familygame

Gather up your troops and set a time and space for simply playing a game together. There are two somewhat challenging parts to your task today: the first is finding a time that will suit your whole family to be at home together and the second is finding a game that your whole family can play. The key to the first challenge is planning - identify a day and a time well in advance that you know will suit everyone. The second challenge will just take a bit of thought. Do not look for the perfect game but for any game you can think of that will have a role for everyone, bearing in mind that the focus is not on the game per se. It is about the playing, which is done together as a family. Try a game that is simple, does not involve technology and will give plenty of laughter. Some suggestions are Monopoly, Twister, Charades, You're a Star, Blind Date, Cluedo, or 20 Questions. Now, let the games begin!

WHY AM I DOING THIS?

To put it very simply, you are engaging in family play as it is a fundamental trait of happy families. When playing a game together, all family members become equal. There are no 'parent' or 'child' roles honored and everyone adopts their own roles. Additionally, playing a game with one another allows for time where the parent and child can be engaged together in the same process. This is a rarity nowadays as usually a parent and a child will be engaged in very different thought processes throughout the day. Research has found that those who participate in family play show significant improvement in family relations.[93] It is not surprising that children find family play beneficial since, when involved in the game, the whole family are communicating through play, which is the natural language of the child. However, it is not only children who reap the rewards as research shows that parents report greater satisfaction in family life when they are more involved in activities, such as family games, that are not done as part of a daily routine but contribute to a surprising novelty for the family.[94]

#kidsday53

#evaluate2educate

Build upon your child's evaluation skills – help them identify relevant pros and cons

#evaluate2educate

WHAT DO I NEED TO DO?

The first step in promoting evaluation skills is to assist your child in a reflection exercise. You can do this by picking out an activity your child engaged in and asking them to think about how it was. Next, suggest that they think of ways they would like to change their experience if they were to do it again and, then, to pick out the good and not-so-good aspects of the experience. Once a child has learned the skill of reflective evaluation, they are ready to move on to evaluating something that is due to take place in the future. This process is useful to practice in making a decision about going somewhere or not – pick an event and ask your child to select the positive and the negative features about going there. If your child is not able to verbalize their thoughts, picture aids can help with the process.

WHY AM I DOING THIS?

Proficient evaluation and reflection skills are important tools in aiding the development of a child's language, thinking, social, and creative competencies. By encouraging a child to reflect upon their experiences, we are allowing them to go to a deeper level of thought processing by scrutinizing beyond what they have just done. Instead, your child is drawn to attend to what they have learned from their experiences and what they would like to learn from such an experience in the future. This is a skill central to becoming proficient and independent thinkers. Research shows that reflection consolidates knowledge so it can be generalized to other situations, thereby leading to further prediction and evaluation. By encouraging your child to express their intentions and evaluate their actions, you equip your child with the thinking skills they need for later educational success and favorable outcomes in adult life.[95]

INDEPENDENCE BUILDING

#snapit

Snap it!

#snapit

WHAT DO I NEED TO DO?

In a time where we have a camera at hand for most of the day, why not make the most of it and capture some of the more simple moments that your child has. Rather than focus on the elements of beauty in the background or the perfect outfit to dress him/her in, the aim today is to capture the really basic moments of your child investigating a ladybird or coloring in a picture they have drawn. Oftentimes, many of the photos parents take for social media are designed to attain 'likes' or compliments from friends. Today, you are asked to take a few photos of the more natural moments that define the everyday experience of your family's life – chocolate stains, messy hair and grazed knees are all a part of that. It is always necessary to take notice of the tiny moments of beauty that do not fit into the 'conventional beauty' box. #100happydays4kids cherishes this kind of beauty!

WHY AM I DOING THIS?

When flicking through photos, it is important for us to be mindful of what real beauty is and not get caught up on what society dictates beauty should look like. Teaching children the real meaning of beauty is fundamental to their development. The stain on their face and messy hair are not important factors; the beauty is in the experience of building a sand-castle, the learning that happens in the process, the emotions that are attached, and the memories created. Never lose grasp of the importance of what childhood is all about and never fail to capture this in your photos. Showing your children what real beauty is will help create a positive self-image not obsessed with 'the ideal', which is a central tenet to adaptive functioning in children.[96] Children and adolescents with a positive self-image are more likely to accept responsibility, deal with frustration effectively, attempt new experiences, and offer help to their peers.[97]

FUNDAMENTAL PARENTING SKILL

#chalkplay

Chalk play

#chalkplay

WHAT DO I NEED TO DO?

Today, you will help your child put their creative stamp on the outdoor communal world. All you need is a piece of chalk and an outdoor cement or stone surface. Once you have found your creative spot, you must tell your child 'Let's draw with chalk!' and do not explain anything more. You may need to start the drawing yourself to ensure your child knows that they do have your permission. However, once started, take the lead from your child. They may give you a section of your own or they may want you to join in and create the area with them. If you have a number of children, they may all want you to join them in different ways. Just do the best you can to meet these varying needs.

WHY AM I DOING THIS?

Sharing a creative experience with your child will enhance your bonding. An added feature of this experience is that the drawing is child-led and this happens on a publically accessible canvas. However, they are secure in the knowledge that they can easily remove the drawing as the chalk will just wipe away. Drawing outdoors with chalk is an ideal way of promoting outdoor play with children who may prefer to be indoors, whilst remaining respectful to their natural play tendencies. Children often find it difficult to express themselves publicly and this provides them with a safe and non-permanent means of practicing this. Where there is more than one child involved, it provides them with the opportunity to utilize shared spaces in a manner that is respectful to others' boundaries and an opportunity to engage in cooperative interactions. Simply engaging in this artistic process, where nothing is expected of the child, will not only reveal a reflection of the child's inner self, but will help to shape the formation of the inner self too.[98]

#childrensmenu

Children's menu

#childrensmenu

WHAT DO I NEED TO DO?

The task today may take some preparation as you are asked to prepare all of your child's favorite food for every meal – breakfast, lunch and dinner. Such that they do not order lots and lots of chocolate for all three meals, you may implement the rule that only breakfast foods may be used for breakfast or a minimum of one vegetable or piece of fruit of their choice must be included in each meal. This can be planned by the child themselves the day before or you may help them think about all the options that they have open to them. Show your child all that is available in the cupboard and refrigerator and let them decide what they think will work best. It is up to you whether or not you want to offer to bring your child on a trip to the shopping center to buy some extra ingredients or to challenge them by having them think of what they can create with whatever food is there.

WHY AM I DOING THIS?

This activity today is very much in line with one of the most fundamental messages of this book, which is the promotion of your child's independence. The activity is broken down into numerous sub-tasks of independence promotion including deciding what meals they will plan for the following day (breakfast, lunch and dinner or brunch, dinner and tea), what they will have for each of the meals, what ingredients they will add to each meal, and how they can help prepare for, produce or serve the food themselves. They must also decide what they can realistically produce using the ingredients available in the pantry or what foods they need to add to the shopping list. You can see now how this task encourages self-expression, self-fulfilment, self-direction, and making individual decisions.[99]

FAMILY ATTACHMENT AND BONDING

#kidsday57

#mykidsrecipes

Today, I will create a recipe book with my child

#mykidsrecipes

WHAT DO I NEED TO DO?

Identify, with your child, their favorite things to eat for breakfast, lunch, dinner, dessert and as snacks. Then, using pictures from the internet, from magazines, from your own creations or from food-packaging, create a scrapbook of the recipes you want to produce. Help your child design these recipes by identifying the ingredients and equipment needed for each dish and the method that needs to be followed. This should be created in a manner accessible to the child so pictures can be used to guide the younger children through the steps. You can even tailor the recipe book to each child, by including pictures of them with the full set of ingredients and at each stage of the cooking process and then enjoying the meal at the end.

WHY AM I DOING THIS?

Many children leave the family home with little knowledge of how to cook for themselves. You can avoid this happening to your child by starting the task of showing them how to prepare meals early, thus, empowering them with the ability to provide for themselves naturally. Research has found that participating in cooking classes results in the acquisition of more positive eating habits and in children eating more fruit and vegetables. Research focusing on young children participating in cooking clubs found that learning how to cook improved the children's ability to recognize healthier foods and increased their desire to eat these healthier foods.[100]

INDEPENDENCE BUILDING

#100 HAPPY DAYS 4 KIDS

#kidsday58

#takeyourtime

Take your time

#takeyourtime

WHAT DO I NEED TO DO?

If you take the time to stop and notice, you will be surprised by how many times parents and teachers tell their children and students to 'Hurry up', 'Come one' and 'Do it faster'. Can you remember a time when you were doing your best but someone was continually nagging at you to hurry, hurry, hurry?! It is not a very pleasant feeling and, although there are times when parents feel late, frustrated and burdened by fifteen million tasks and their child looks like they are taking their sweet time, we need to take a look at this. Today you are asked to catch yourself before you feel a 'hurry up' coming, and breathe. Instead, tell your child 'Take your time'. Allow your child those few extra minutes eating their dinner or getting dressed and those few extra seconds getting out of the car or tidying up their toys. You will notice that the world will not end and your child will feel less stressed.

WHY AM I DOING THIS?

Parents need to be mindful of the amount of stress and pressure that young children are placed under on a daily basis. As well as learning social norms and a language with which to communicate, youngsters also have to cope with an education system which challenges them every day. As such, children should be respected and given as much time as they need to complete tasks in order to learn new skills. Research has shown that a child will succeed in learning to the extent that s/he spends the amount of time that s/he requires to learn.[101] Unfortunately, research has also shown that, as well as the intellectual strain placed upon young people by the demands of the educational setting, parents also demand high levels of achievement.[102] This study found that dissatisfied parents felt as though their children were not utilizing their full capability and making enough effort. Allowing the child time to complete their little tasks and learning reduces stress placed on them, which is recommended as a positive parenting technique because an array of studies have clearly linked stress to negative child and adolescent consequences, including depression, anxiety, suicide attempts, antisocial behavior and health problems.[103]

FUNDAMENTAL PARENTING SKILL

#walkintherain

Walk in the rain

#walkintherain

WHAT DO I NEED TO DO?

We often look out on those dark rainy days and consider venturing outside to be an impossibility – the cold, the wet, the misery. However, why not throw on the raingear and go for a walk? Providing you and your child have protective raingear and waterproof footwear, participating in this new sensory experience need not be a negative experience. Splashing in puddles, listening to the raindrops on your hood and feeling the sensation of rain on your face can be fun and relaxing. You and your child may be newly experiencing this type of nature walk but it is never too late. In an age where televisions and social media seem to be taking over, we often find ourselves looking for excuses to not exercise or take time to explore nature. However, there is nothing more rewarding than to see your child explore on an imaginary adventure or celebrate after finding a beautiful flower or exciting new cubby. And it costs nothing!

WHY AM I DOING THIS?

Aside from being physically advantageous for a growing child, embracing the weather and taking sufficient natural outdoor exercise is also psychologically beneficial,[104] with a significant endorphin-release resulting in that 'feel-good factor'. Studies have shown that exercise is also effective for the enhancement of cognitive performance in young people. Research suggests that both progressive muscle relaxation and large muscle exercise are effective for treating hyperactive, impulsive youths.[105] In order to ascertain which setting may be the most effective for relaxation and exercise, you will need to take into consideration what types of areas are in your locality for a fun, energetic and relaxing family nature walk. Research has found that a coniferous forest setting was one of the most favored to evoke a positive reaction.[106]

ACTIVITY-BASED LEARNING

#beingbeautifulyou

What's it like to be you?

#beingbeautifulyou

WHAT DO I NEED TO DO?

Today, you are asked to have a conversation with your child exploring what it is like for them to be who they are – a child, a son, a sister, a nephew and a grand-child. You are also asked to share what it is like for you to be you – a mother, a wife, a single parent, a sister, a son, an aunt and a teacher. Listen to everything that your child has to say about this, whether it may be positive or negative as there is so much to learn from the questions you might not normally pose. You might learn how your middle child often feels as though they receive less attention than the other two, how your nine-year-old feels as though they deserve more independence and responsibility, or how your seventeen-year-old loves spending time with his Grand-dad.

WHY AM I DOING THIS?

For a child to explain what it is like to be them, they need to really think about themselves in a way they may never have done before. They need to learn to explain something that is so obvious to them that they had never needed to think about it too much or verbalize it before. Now, when considering themselves, they need to compare what they know to what you know and fill in the gaps. This style of thinking is complex for a child but is extremely beneficial as it facilitates their understanding that they are completely different from everyone else. Oftentimes, we can be feeling an emotion without realizing it and it is only when a therapist focuses questions around our emotions that we recognize how we are doing. Your child does not need a therapist to learn this new task because you are now fully equipped. This task promotes a sense of identity and emotional independence for your child, which are both important developmental tasks that everyone needs.[107]

FAMILY ATTACHMENT AND BONDING

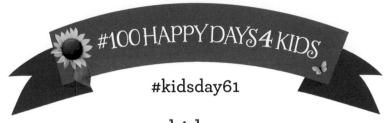

#mykidspeers

Have your child's friend over to your house – watch their interactions and learn about the impact of your parenting style

WHAT DO I NEED TO DO?

Invite over to your house one of each of your child's friends. You might want to do this on separate days depending on how many kids you and your home can cope with. When the friend is at your house, simply watch how your child interacts with him/her. Do not interrupt or guide them where possible, but simply watch. Today, you are watching your child's peer interactions to learn about what kind of impact your parenting is having. Listen to the way your child speaks to their friend, watch how they manage tasks together, see what they do if a conflict arises, check how they trust in each other and do all of this with an open reflective mind. When the friend is gone home, ask your child how their day was with their friend and help them to reflect on their peer interactions. This joint reflection exercise will provide you both with opportunities for learning. It is at this point that you can guide your child to thinking about what they might do differently in the future with a friend. You are teaching them how to be reflective and how to learn from interactions with others, a key concept in becoming an independent competent social being.

WHY AM I DOING THIS?

A child's innate traits are shaped, strengthened or counteracted by the child's relationships and experiences. Some children may be naturally pre-disposed to find it difficult to manage life's stresses; however, supportive responsive adults in a low stress, accepting environment has been shown to reduce this potential difficulty.[108] Research has identified five building blocks of human relationships – which are what you want to foster in your child. **Trust** is a confident belief in oneself and in others that allows a young child to explore the unknown with the security of knowing they will be provided with the support and encouragement they need. **Autonomy** is the capacity for independence, identity, exploration and thinking that prompts a child to explore their world independently. **Initiative** is the capacity for children to begin and then follow through on a task. **Empathy** is the capacity that allows children to understand others' feelings by relating them to feelings that they themselves have had. Empathy helps children form relationships and develop a sense of belonging. **Self-confidence** is the capacity to believe in one's own ability to accomplish tasks, communicate and contribute positively to society.[109]

#100 HAPPY DAYS 4 KIDS

#kidsday62

#thankyou

Thank you

#thankyou

WHAT DO I NEED TO DO?

Today, yourself and your child are asked to create and design ten 'Thank You' notes, letters or mini-cards. These can be as simple or as extravagant as you both want and can have personalized messages if you know in advance who you will be distributing these to. If your child has a neighbor who recently gave him/her a lift to school, maybe you could both drop in and show how thankful you both are. Showing gratitude to those who are a part of your lives is a wonderful way of setting a good example for your child. Alternatively, you could simply design ten notes, letters or mini-cards that are more generic and not personal, but you could give them out as people help you throughout the day. The lady who helps you fill your bags might deserve one or perhaps the man in the park might have earned one for telling you that you forgot your hat. As always, this activity is best if child-directed and centered around activities and people important to him/her.

WHY AM I DOING THIS?

Training your child to always be appreciative and thankful for the small things is a life skill, essential for life satisfaction. Scientific evidence for the effects of gratitude on our well-being has been gathering rapidly over the past few years.[110] Results from a number of studies has shown that gratitude enhances a person's holistic well-being, including their level of life satisfaction and happiness.[111,112,113] Fredrickson[114] stipulates that gratitude is responsible for mutual humanitarianism, which is the unselfish thoughtfulness resulting in lasting friendship and social attachments. Overall well-being can be improved through using gratitude as one recognizes that social resources were drawn upon during difficult times, for example, when you had a friend's shoulder to cry on. Showing gratitude increases the likelihood that these same social resources will provide support again when necessary in the future.

FUNDAMENTAL PARENTING SKILL

#pressaflower

Press a flower

#pressaflower

This may be an activity that you have done with your child before but the advantages are just fantastic so please share this experience with your child today. During Spring and Summer, we are spoilt with a wealth of beautiful flowers, which range from dainty and pastel to eye-catching and vibrant. You and your child are asked to decide on a beautiful flower together and pick it. Talk to your child about why this is the flower they want and where s/he wants to put it in your home. At home, lay some newspaper on the table and place the flower on the paper facing upwards. Arrange it so that, when squashed, you will be able to see its center. Place a layer of newspaper on top and squash with many heavy books. In order to dry the flower even quicker, place it in a hot press or somewhere that is continually warm and very dry, but not hot. After a week, you will uncover the flower, place it in a frame painted by you both, write your names and the date underneath, and hang it up in a place fitting for such a unique and wondrous piece of art.

WHY AM I DOING THIS?

The drive to get more children playing and exploring outside is based on the assumption that children today are spending more time indoors than their predecessors;[115] however, there have also been research findings published which clearly stipulate a recent decline in participation in outdoor leisure and recreation.[116] This may be related to the concurrent increase in Information and Communications Technology (ICT) in the lives of young children, which includes mobile phones, laptops and tablets with portable entertainment systems.[117] Allowing children to wander through a wild natural field and pick a flower that they love is such a simple gift, but has so many physical, emotional and sensory benefits. Creating a piece of art with this flower means that your child can forever be reminded of the day they felt connected with the world on a level so unlike anything they could experience using technology.

ACTIVITY-BASED LEARNING

#minithanksgivingday

Mini-thanksgiving day

#minithanksgivingday

The exercise today will not take long to complete but should result in food for thought for both yourself and your child. The aim is to take some time to appreciate as many things as you can about your life. It is recommended that you and your child sit down and make a list of ten things each that you are grateful for. An example might be, 'I am thankful for always having fresh milk in my fridge' or 'I'm grateful for having a baby sister'. Talk to your child about what life would be like without these things or people in your life. It might be an idea to pin these ideas up somewhere where you both often pass by so that this list serves as a reminder. It can always be added to in the future or replaced by newer items.

WHY AM I DOING THIS?

Gratitude is defined as the emotional response deriving from the perception of a positive personal outcome, including recognition, acknowledgement and/or appreciation of the receipt of a benefit.[118] Interestingly, researchers in the popular field of positive psychology, regard and emphasize that the act of regularly being thankful does contribute and enhance overall wellbeing and promotes higher levels of happiness among all individuals.[119] There is no greater joy than accounting for all the small aspects of your life that bring you pleasure, which often far outweigh the negative. It sometimes feels as though our woes are overwhelming but forcing your brain to break this negative thought-cycle and to focus instead on the positive gravitates you toward feeling a little bit more grateful for the small things, like coffee and cake. Enjoy this task!

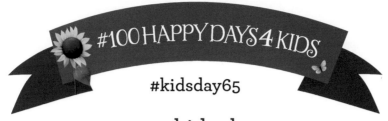
Help your child plan their own day, week, month or year

#mykidsplan

WHAT DO I NEED TO DO?

Planning ahead is a valuable life skill and a quality that children often tend to naturally possess, especially when they see their parents modelling this behavior. Today, you are going to engage in your child's planning to nurture this important developmental tool. To get started, provide your child with tangible options to help them make the initial steps. For example, ask your child to choose what game you will play after dinner and encourage them to set it up. You can then move to more abstract plans like discussing what the day will entail in the morning or planning what the week ahead will look like on a Sunday evening. Helping your child plan is a different process to telling your child what will be happening. For your child to learn how to plan, they must be involved in this process by establishing what they have to do on a day, which helps a child to prioritize and set realistic goals. Once your child has acquired this ability to think about what will happen in the future, you can encourage them to elaborate on their own plans, listen to a plan that they are making no matter how small, and help them record their plans using words, a calendar or a picture-planner like in the template available from your member area of www.100happydays4kids.com.

WHY AM I DOING THIS?

By helping your child to execute their own plans you are promoting the development of metacognition, which is the psychological term that defines higher-level thinking and problem-solving skills. Metacognitive development takes place when children are encouraged to reflect, predict, question, and hypothesize. When we engage children in planning, we encourage them to identify their goals and consider the options for achieving them. For example, they might consider what they will do, where they will do it, what materials they will use, who they will do it with, how long it will take, and whether they will need help. As such, planning involves deciding on actions and predicting interactions, recognizing problems and proposing solutions, as well as anticipating consequences and reactions.[120]

#managingdisappointment

Managing disappointment

#managingdisappointment

WHAT DO I NEED TO DO?

Children often have huge disappointments to deal with when their demands or requests are not met. Your task today is to teach your child the difference between 'demands' and 'preferences' and to change their demands into preferences. This is similar to the difference between 'needs' and 'wants'. There is a sense of entitlement that comes from demanding something; however, expressing your preference does not suggest that you will attain that toy or food. It is a part of your task today to gently explain to your child in an empathetic tone that there will be times when they cannot get everything they WANT and that anger is not a reaction that will progress the situation in any way. Explain to them about a time when you did not get something you wanted, how you reacted in a non-aggressive manner and how this was much more progressive and acceptable.

WHY AM I DOING THIS?

Anger grows from not managing disappointment effectively and can be detrimental if allowed to continue without parental intervention. There is no need for any child to feel anger once parents listen to their child's emotions and explain why certain actions have been or cannot be taken. When not dealt with effectively, anger has the potential to cause much more significant harm to the child and others. Externalizing difficulties in older children and adolescents, such as anti-social behavior, are associated with a much higher level of anger than more submissive emotions like sadness.[121] Changing the way the child views the world can help them to understand that it is not always possible to have something they want. Facilitating the child to soothe their own disappointment is remarkably beneficial as it is an essential life-skill they can utilize for the rest of their lives.

FUNDAMENTAL PARENTING SKILL

#kidsday67

#cloudplay

Cloud play

#cloudplay

WHAT DO I NEED TO DO?

Parents, try this task when you have a dry cloudy day out because you are asked to lie on the ground with your child and watch the skies. You are both asked to pick out and show one another ten animals, people or objects in the clouds above. Children have a very different way of understanding their environment and this will allow you to see the world through your child's eyes and understand their unique and innocent rationality. You may notice that this task seems easier for your child as all children have an intrinsic curiosity and an incredibly active imagination, which usually fade over time into adulthood. It is important to take parenting back to the bare basics, to when all we had was nature and plenty of time.

WHY AM I DOING THIS?

This is a simple task for parents to carry out with their children in order to flex that 'imagination muscle'. The imagination is likened to a muscle in that the more it is exercised, the more proficient and easier it is for the child to use at their own will. Encouraging your child to view fluffy white clouds and to think about what they might be able to visualize is both stimulating and relaxing as the task is carried out very much at their own pace. Also, they have complete freedom and only the boundaries of their own imaginations can limit their musings. As such, this is a fantastic activity for the development of your child's self-expression and self-identity.[122] Finally, being together with your child in such a natural and remote way is almost transcendental in that all of your senses are being treated to the experience of the ground underneath, the sky above and the fresh air all around. Bask in this activity and enjoy it!

#kidsday68

#familystory

Create your family's story

#familystory

WHAT DO I NEED TO DO?

Today, you are going to create your own family story, which you can do this using miniature toys, puppets, plushes, dolls, kitchen utensils, cushions, music and colors, but you can basically use anything you have to hand! Make sure that everyone understands that the story will be in 'pretend' form, nobody is themselves in the story and that they can take the story anywhere their imagination brings them. Set the scene by first gathering together every member of the family and explain that you are all going to do a story together and then decide what props or tools everyone wants to get. You can use a full room to act out your story or you can do it on a smaller scale on a table, in a sand tray or even leaning over a bath of water. Then, all you have to do is start the story and give a nod to the next family member to continue on when you are finished your first line. This is a great way of stepping into the mind-set of child, but it is done using the safe realm of the imagination. Older children and adults find it harder to lend themselves to the world of the pretend, but it comes with time and practice. On the other hand, younger children naturally possess this ability.

WHY AM I DOING THIS?

Storytelling is a developmentally sensitive tool that can be used to elicit children's thoughts, identify their distortions, and help them to make sense of their world more accurately.[123] The use of stories in the manner described above is a productive means for communicating with children because it provides a medium through which a real message can be presented to children in a manner accessible to them. Storytelling conducted by the whole family provides an opportunity for family members to form an interactive bond as story-tellers and listeners. By encouraging each member to take their turn, you are strengthening the relationship between the parent and the child. Additionally, the presentation of a story in this manner is an opportunity for the child to form a relationship with the characters or to identify with a character, as created by other family members, which tends to reflect some aspect of their personalities, one that the child themselves may not often see.

FAMILY ATTACHMENT AND BONDING

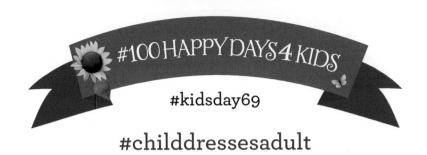

#childdressesadult

Child dresses adult

#childdressesadult

WHAT DO I NEED TO DO?

You may need a strong coffee and a little early morning pep-talk today as you are about to be paid back for all those mornings your child did NOT want to wear those boots or jeans. It is advisable to fulfill this task on a day you have no outdoor chores to run. Inform your child that they will be picking out both of your outfits today. Ensure that you are prepared because you will have committed yourself to fulfilling this promise to you child. As such, when your child picks out that pineapple shirt and those purple velvet slacks, well...tough luck. This may allow you to realize how valuable our personal preferences and individual freedom are, which we often inadvertently take from our children (especially, when in a rush). However, the main aim of the activity today is to offer your child a little task encouraging independence and expression.

WHY AM I DOING THIS?

What does fostering independence mean to your child? Well, it refers to all the components of human functioning that involve being physically and psychologically separate from everyone else and being capable of maintaining oneself in a self-sufficient manner. Overprotection or overly applying rules can stifle a child's natural progression toward independence and make the natural break from the family more difficult in the long term. The modern culture of today celebrates and promotes independence and all of the determinants of this value, including self-expression, self-fulfillment, being self-directed, and being able to make individual decisions and define oneself separately from peers.[124] Allowing your child to see that their choices matter and have consequences in your world by allowing them to pick your clothes symbolizes the freedom and expression that they will have more and more of as they grow older.

#100 HAPPY DAYS 4 KIDS

#kidsday70

#childsday

Child's day

#childsday

This task is best prepared for a few days before, when you are asked to make mental notes about all of your child's favorite things to do, listen to, watch, eat and drink. Try not to make it obvious as you will want for this day to be a surprise for them. Often, when parents organize a day for their children, they arrange it based on what other parents have recommended or on reviews or deals they have read about. However, you may be surprised about how easy it is to plan a day around your child's favorite activities. Often, it is more about who children spend their day with, what they have for lunch, and how much freedom they are allowed to enjoy. On the planned day, you are asked to spend the day fully engaged in spoiling your child with all of their most favorite activities.

WHY AM I DOING THIS?

Most parents nowadays have the burden of conflicting career and family commitments, which they can never seem to resolve in any harmonious way. Not only do parents feel as though it is difficult to spend enough time with their children but they also struggle to feel as though this time is adequately characterized by love and nurturance. However, research has shown that when parents do spend 'quality time' with their children, they feel as though tasks which enhance the quality their time together contributed to the parent/child bond, as well as to their child's overall holistic well-being.[125] This is all despite the fact that these parents had acknowledged spending inadequate amounts of quality time with their children, which highlights how even smaller amounts of quality time can significantly improve parent-child relationships.

FUNDAMENTAL PARENTING SKILL

#fourseasonsautumn

Four seasons – Autumn

#fourseasonsautumn

WHAT DO I NEED TO DO?

Today, we will share Vivaldi's Four Seasons with our child again, specifically the first movement of Autumn (Allegro) [please note: the first and third movements are both named Allegro but it is the first we recommend]. At this stage, your child will have had two opportunities to practice how to use their imagination to create a piece of art about two different seasons and should find this a little easier than before. Conduct this task as you did Spring and Summer, making any modifications if necessary. If you had not practiced talking to your child about what they created before, that is your task today. As always, lead by example yourself and talk to your child about what you saw, felt, smelled, tasted and heard during the piece of music. Point to colors, objects and people in your art which show and explain how you felt. Ask about what they thought and felt about it, as well as all of the different sensory information.

WHY AM I DOING THIS?

Just like Vivaldi's Spring and Summer, the first benefit of this task is that it promotes relaxation and allows you and your child to take a break from the real world for a section of the day. Conceptualizing, processing and explaining the information your child is experiencing through their senses of hearing, sight, smell, taste and touch is an exercise in practicing purposeful awareness, which allows one to feel centered, more in control of their emotions and more relaxed.[126] Transferring these experiences on to a tangible medium is referred to as 'mindful art' and allows others to see what your child could never have explained in words, particularly if they are younger. Having a method of expressing emotions facilitates your child unloading their emotions and helps them to cope in a safe, self-directed and independent way.

ACTIVITY-BASED LEARNING

Build a fort

#buildafort

WHAT DO I NEED TO DO?

Today, you are asked to take a step or two back in time to when it was the best fun in the whole wide world to get all the cushions, pillows, beanbags, blankets and sheets in the house and make the biggest, most incredible fort anyone had ever seen. You were king/queen of this castle and could play inside your fort for hours and hours on end. Usually, an adult would come along and put a halt to your gallop but you will not be the party-pooper for your child today. Today! YOU will jump right in with your child and be construction manager if they need one. You will help guard, maintain, or defend your fort, if your child requires this assistance. Alternatively, their babies might just need an extra maid or they may require assistance with their beauty routine. Whatever the case, spend some quality time being positively and fully engaged with your child in your fort and, by all means, feel ridiculous!

WHY AM I DOING THIS?

According to Pauline Johnson, professor of art, "Great value of the arts lies in the opportunity provided for the development of the imagination which needs to be exercised and nourished".[127] There is no need to go outside the door of your house in order to make art with your child: children are the most efficient and imaginative of all age-groups and will surprise you with their inventiveness, no doubt. It is intuitively engrained in the child to transform basic materials such as cushions and blankets into manmade structures even world-class architects would be envious of. It is up to the parent, in this teacher/colleague role, to supply the child with enough objects of interest for the child to maintain stimulation and learn new rules about physics, patterns and textures. You may be surprised by how many hours children can enjoy this simple type of imaginative play and forget about technology!

#nonegativesentencesday

No negative sentences day

#nonegativesentencesday

WHAT DO I NEED TO DO?

If the task today is successful, the title will be the only negative sentence you will come across. Parents do not often pay attention to what is being said during daily conversations with their children and to do so at all times would, quite frankly, be exhausting. However, as care-givers, it comes with the territory that a vast amount of speech is spent delivering warnings, cautions and directions. Today, you are asked to pay attention to the messages you are delivering to your child and try to convey the same messages in a positive framework and explain why. An example of this may be to say 'Can you walk, please, because you might trip up?' instead of 'Don't run!' Notice the difference? Same message, different delivery.

WHY AM I DOING THIS?

One of the tenets of a phenomenon known as 'positive parenting' is that parents may correct the mistakes of the child so long as they provide logical, rational, and reasonable reasons.[128] This routine encourages the child to be independent, by allowing them to take part in their own activities and lessen the amount of advice and help sought from parents.[129] By framing the sentence in a positive manner, care-givers can lessen the amount of restrictive parenting they exert, allowing children to have more control and independence over what they want to do with that information. While poor parenting practices are consistently associated with disruptive behavior,[130] a more positive parenting practice is considered a protective factor for children.[131]

Take some time today to pause and reflect on the happiness levels of your family as a whole now that you are three quarters of the way into your challenge

#pause2reflect

WHAT DO I NEED TO DO?

Focus on how much happier **your whole family** seem to be feeling now compared to seventy-four days ago.

DOCUMENT & SHARE

Why not document your experience on **www.100happydays4kids.com** where you can share your experience with others and see how people from around the world are benefiting from engaging in this challenge?

Do not forget to share your journey of happiness with your friends too!

#kidsday75

#shoutoutloud

Shout! Out! Loud!

#shoutoutloud

WHAT DO I NEED TO DO?

The aim of the game today is to take the time to visit a peaceful place, like a woods, the middle of a field or the coastline, and shout as loud as you can. You will then encourage your child to do the same. The only requisite today is that you shout as many times as you can or need to in order to feel some relief. This exercise can be great after a hectic day in order to release pent-up angst. Consider how silly you all look. Look at one another's face while screaming and have a laugh. Sharing this experience and taking part in a new silly activity facilitates the bonding of your family unit. The next time you pass that glade or shore you will be carried back to the time you all had fun there together. Document your feelings afterwards on www.100happydays4kids.com and see how they compare to other families' experiences.

WHY AM I DOING THIS?

Research has shown that, when people share a past of experiences like families commonly do, they can generate humor by toying with qualities they have developed together.[132] As a result, sharing more happy experiences together as a family leads to more funny references, jokes and good times among members into the future. For example, although rocketing down the huge waterslide on holidays was fun, the giggles on the plane home while flicking through the pictures are just as valuable. This extension of the fun shared experience leads to the development of more positive relationships within the family. Children can be very impressed when they see their parent doing something funny and ridiculous and this positive regard has an influence on the overall impression they have. Creating and sharing frequent happy experiences within your family will result in better inter-family relations in the long-term.

ACTIVITY-BASED LEARNING

#kidsday76

#otherfamilies

Spend time as a family with another family

#otherfamilies

WHAT DO I NEED TO DO?

Have a look around and see if there is another family that your family could spend some time with. They can be work colleagues, the family of your child's friends, a family from your own relatives, a family of old school friends, or families that you may meet at family events. All you are required to do is simply spend time as a family in the company of another family. Have discussions with other parents and allow your child to interact with other children but you are all still in the context of the family unit, enjoying time together with others.

WHY AM I DOING THIS?

Fundamentally, you are doing this to be able to socialize as a family which involves more than being out together as a family. Instead, it involves interacting in a social manner with others and your family, whereby you are bonding as a unit, as well as having the opportunity to spend time with others. Research has formed a firm establishment of the positive relationship between family recreation and a number of family and individual outcomes, including satisfaction, stability, cohesion, and child development.[133] Our culture does not often set the scene for this: teenagers tend to socialize with other teenagers, parents tend to socialize with each other or with their own peer groups and young children tend to have play-dates. Society almost expects the family to separate and only socialize like that. By socializing as a family unit, children get to see their parents in a different light – they see that Mammy or Daddy is a parent to them but that they are also a friend to someone else. It also gives children the opportunity to see other types of family units and appreciate diversity. They will learn that things are done differently in other families and, once you are accepting of that, they will be too. This helps to broaden their understanding of the world. Parents too can learn a lot from spending time with other families as a family as it helps you to step outside of your own parenting world and appreciate it from the outside in.

#scaffoldyourway

Focus on the process of scaffolding

#scaffoldyourway

WHAT DO I NEED TO DO?

To assist your child in becoming a competent and independent learner, try to incorporate the method of scaffolding into your ways of teaching your child. To do this, you must pick a topic that you feel is important for your child to acquire further knowledge about at this present time, based on your evaluation of their needs, as well as the cues they provide you with. Once you have identified this area, observe the child's existing competencies and aim to build on those. You can do this by guiding your child to the next stage of learning, by incorporating and building upon their existing competencies. For example, if your child is able to build three blocks high, encourage your child to build to this height (existing competency) and demonstrate how additional blocks can be added (guiding to the next stage). However, only demonstrate this a couple of times and always follow from the child's existing competencies. A point to remember is that you can guide your child, but only they will truly acquire knowledge themselves, in their own time and at their own pace.

WHY AM I DOING THIS?

Bruner coined the term 'scaffolding',[134] which was derived from Vygotsky's theory of social development,[135] to represent an important model of learning, whereby the present knowledge level of a child is identified and they are assisted in acquiring knowledge just above this level. Next, the adult begins to remove supports until the child is proficient and the adult reengages when the time is right for the child to progress further. This is an important method for parents to adopt as it demonstrates the necessary balance between guiding and teaching your child, but yet allows them the space to fully master a skill themselves. Through adopting this model, we are allowing the child to be viewed as a being of intelligence, a co-constructor of knowledge, as opposed to a blank slate that needs elaborate adult intervention to acquire knowledge.[136]

INDEPENDENCE BUILDING

#kidsday78

#mirroring

Be your child's mirror and let your child be your mirror

#mirroring

WHAT DO I NEED TO DO?

The task today involves the dual process of mirroring your child's behaviors and observing how your behaviors are being mirrored by your child. To mirror your child's behaviors, simply interact with the world in the same manner as your child. When your child engages in an activity, you do it the same way. For example, if your child is on their phone whilst watching television, you do the same thing and if your child is painting a picture, you sit and paint the same picture at the same pace as your child. The second part of the task requires you to observe your child's behaviors and actions to identify any elements of your own behaviors that your child is mirroring. This can be a more difficult process than it initially sounds, as it requires you to be open to becoming aware of your own behaviors as you see them being displayed by your child.

WHY AM I DOING THIS?

Engaging in the process of mirroring your child's activities will provide you, as a parent, with an insight into your child's experience of the world, thus, deepening your ability to empathize with your child. Research has shown that as parents' empathetic behavior increases, levels of parenting-related stress significantly decrease, as do problems with children's behaviors.[137] The interactions between a parent and a child form the ideal opportunity for learning. As you observe how your child mirrors your behaviors and your actions, you become aware of the importance of behaving and acting in a manner that you wish them to experience. Research has shown that simply observing an action being carried out can have the same neurological reactions as carrying out the action yourself.[138]

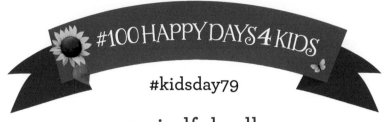
#mindfulwalk

Today, I will go for a mindful walk with my family

#mindfulwalk

WHAT DO I NEED TO DO?

Take some time out of the normal hectic routine to get the whole family together to go for a walk. This can be done at any time of the year as each season brings its own beautiful surrounds. When picking a place for your walk try to choose somewhere that allows optimum access to nature like a forest, beach, woodland, park or a large garden. The most important thing is that you can be together as a family in nature, without the everyday distractions of modern living. Make your walk a mindful one by focusing on your surroundings. For instance, a walk in a forest during Autumn can be mindful by breathing in the Autumnal scents through your nose, by listening to the sounds of the leaves under your feet, by taking in the sights of the array of natural colors on the trees around you, by drawing your attention to the feeling of the crisp air on your skin, and by experiencing a taste of happiness simply from being together.

WHY AM I DOING THIS?

The fact that physical activity results in a more positive mood is reported widely, with a clear association having been found between physical activity and several subjective indicators of well-being.[139] Engaging in a physical exercise activity, such as walking, stimulates the brains sympathetic nervous system and results in higher concentrations of the neurotransmitter, serotonin, which is responsible for increased feelings of happiness and psychological well-being. Many studies, from both survey and experimental research, provide support for the well-publicized statement that 'exercise makes you feel good'.[140] Additionally, going for a mindful walk has the added benefits associated with walking meditation, which can reduce your blood pressure and heart-rate, create feelings of well-being, help sleep quality and patterns, and help you manage stress.[141]

ACTIVITY-BASED LEARNING

#kidsday80

#dressaseachother

Today, my child and I will dress as each other

#dressaseachother

WHAT DO I NEED TO DO?

Are you ready to have some fun with clothes today? A nice benefit of this task is to have every family member see themselves through the eyes of their nearest and dearest. Be warned: this task can bring about some interesting revelations about yourself, so be ready to embrace the good and the bad. Start the task by explaining that everyone will dress up as one another, that there are no rules and that all clothes and props can be used, BUT everyone must take care of one another's items. You begin by having your family dress up as you. When everyone is ready and standing in front of you, open your eyes. Here, you see yourself as your family sees you. Repeat as above until every family member has had a chance at seeing themselves through the eyes of their family.

WHY AM I DOING THIS?

First and foremost, you are doing this to share a laugh and a giggle with your family members, to connect by doing something meaningful together and to give everyone a chance to step into the shoes of everyone else. When you choose clothes to represent someone else, you are highly likely to embody the role of that person and feel, for a moment, what it is like to be them. Secondly, this task helps you learn about your meta-perceptions, which are the ideas you have about the ideas that others have about you. It is a bit of a complicated concept but you will be learning more about the way you think about yourself by looking at how your family sees you. For children, the biggest influence on their development of self-concept is how their primary caregiver sees them and this, in turn, heavily influences how a child expects to be seen by others.[142]

#mindfulmeal

Today, I will encourage my family to eat mindfully

#mindfulmeal

WHAT DO I NEED TO DO?

During mealtime today, you are asked to slow things right down with your child. You are both asked to think about how your food tastes and feels inside your mouth. What temperature is it? What kinds of colors are in your mouth and how are the different foods and tastes mixing? Are the vegetables cooked to your liking and is that butter accentuating the flavors? How does the spaghetti, mushrooms and onions feel? What are the differences between their textures and what do you like about each of them? How are you able to move food around your mouth, yet never bite your tongue? Did you know you could do that? What does it feel like when you take a drink – refreshing, cooling or painful to sensitive teeth? Feel the food travel down your throat after you swallow: what does that feel like? Aim to spend your whole meal just talking about your food.

WHY AM I DOING THIS?

Practicing mindfulness can and should be done at different times and in a variety of situations. Taking time to focus on the sensation of eating results in a focused and purposeful awareness,[143] which allows children to spend more time chewing their food and appreciating mealtime as more than just routine. Viewing food as something to be enjoyed and savored by the senses changes the experience of mealtime into a pleasurable time to look forward to. Spending longer amounts of time eating means that the family can spend more quality time together and this time for food can become a relaxed social event, where members talk about what might be on their mind. Mealtime is actually the best and easiest time to incorporate these mindful and social aspects as it is the one designated time when all members naturally come together.

INDEPENDENCE BUILDING

#respectfulparenting

Today, I will show my nearest and dearest the full respect they deserve

#respectfulparenting

WHAT DO I NEED TO DO?

Most parents would say that they absolutely respect their children; however, sometimes we need to spend time reflecting on this. Today, watch your interactions with your child and ask yourself if you are respecting them in the way that they deserve? Would you be happy with your child showing the same level of respect to others as you show to them? The key to being respectful of your child is treating them, from as soon as they are born, as individuals with minds of their own. Once you are acknowledging this, you are open to finding out what they want, how they like things done and who they are in their own right. When you are in tune with these things, you can parent in a manner that is respectful to who your child is as an individual.

WHY AM I DOING THIS?

Parenting your child in a manner that is respectful of their individuality is referred to as mind-minded parenting, which is essentially attending to the mind of the individual child. Evidence shows that parental mind-related talk with babies as young as six-months-old predicted secure attachments. Mothers who frequently talked to their children in this manner (for example, identifying the child's feelings and discussing the child's emotional needs) were more likely to have securely-attached children by twelve-months-old.[144] Having a secure attachment means that the child is confident that their care-giver is present and available for emotional and physical support when they need it. There is a large body of evidence to support the value of a secure attachment between parent and child. This even extends to how children relate to others, with research showing that children with secure attachments were more likely to show sympathy towards and offer help to other children who were in distress.[145]

FUNDAMENTAL PARENTING SKILL

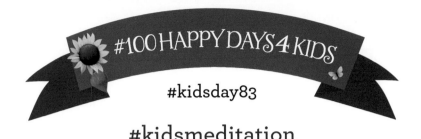

#kidsmeditation

Today, I will meditate with my child

#kidsmeditation

WHAT DO I NEED TO DO?

To introduce this activity to your child, first meet them at their present energy level and guide them down towards a more relaxed state. For example, if the child is jumping around the room, you join them and lead them in pretending you are both monkeys. You then slow the pace, the actions, and the body down gradually by pretending to be bears, snakes, lions and, then, sleeping lion cubs. You then let the child pretend they are blowing up a balloon in their bellies using their breath. Next, get them to focus on their breathing by blowing up the balloon, taking in a breath and letting the air out of the balloon by breathing out. Once the child is centered with their breathing, you can guide them in meditation by playing the #100happydays4kids meditation audio or by slowly and softly reading the #100happydays4kids meditation script, both of which are available in the members' area of our website: www.100happydays4kids.com.

WHY AM I DOING THIS?

Often, children are subject to the same stresses and strains as adults. In addition to this, they absorb others' frustrations and angers and can experience negative emotions more intensely than adults. Children also find it difficult to articulate their problems, so these can manifest into difficult and impulsive behaviors. The main findings of research done on meditation show that it can improve mental abilities (intelligence, creativity, learning ability, memory and academic achievement), health (reductions in stress, anxiety, incidences of ill-health, improved cardiovascular health and increased longevity), and social behavior (improved self-confidence and relationships with others). Quite simply, meditation contributes extensively to human well-being.[146]

#iwillsupportyou

I will support my child

#iwillsupportyou

WHAT DO I NEED TO DO?

Children often have difficulty in talking to their parents as a result of them thinking that their mother or father will not understand, will get angry and will not support them in any way. Worse, they fear their parents will attempt to oppose what they want or need and how they feel. As parents, you are often your child's only source of security and approval and, as such, they can be much stronger and independent people knowing that their parents have their back, no matter what. The task today is to have a chat with your child about this, telling them that there is nothing in this world that could ever change the depth of love you feel for them. Explain that if there was ever anything on their mind they were worried about, please trust that you will do your very best to understand and that you will ALWAYS support them in achieving their dreams. Your role as a parent is not to own this little person, but to facilitate them growing into the best person they can be. They are their own person, with their very own opinions, needs and desires! And, of course, follow this up **when** they do require support for something you might not necessarily agree with.

WHY AM I DOING THIS?

From birth until adulthood, parents are the number one resource for providing children with the support they need for achieving all of their developmental milestones[147], which include physical, social, emotional and intellectual. Many studies show the significance of the parent as a supporter of childhood and adolescent well-being, over peers or any other people.[148] As such, this duty to support your child is one which cannot be under-estimated as it has the ability to protect the child from external factors in their little environments. Allowing the child to know that they always have their primary care-giver's unfaltering support allows that to focus on what they really want and need.

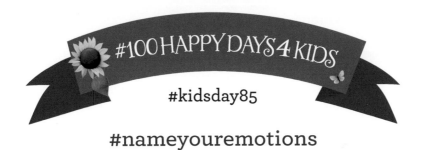

#nameyouremotions

Name your emotions

#nameyouremotions

WHAT DO I NEED TO DO?

There can stigma attached to naming and expressing emotions. However, not naming emotions can lead to children feeling embarrassed, confused and frustrated. It is vital to teach children that it is completely natural to have a range of different emotions at any one time and to encourage them to tell you all about what they feel like. Your task today is to talk to your child when you see him/her feeling overwhelmed or frustrated, come down to their level, and calmly say 'You look like you are finding something difficult. It's natural to feel this way but can you tell me how you are feeling?' Explain to your child that every emotion has a name and that just naming it will help you understand what is going on for him/her. It is also important to note that it is possible for us to experience a blend of many different emotions at any one time. Working through these emotions can result in more effective healing and resolutions to difficulties.

WHY AM I DOING THIS?

It can be difficult for children to recognize and understand different emotions that they might not have felt before. They may not have any idea about what this strange emotion is or why it is happening to them. Emotions such as guilt, embarrassment and jealousy are more complex than happiness and may need to be explained to and explored with a child. The processing skills involved in emotion recognition and understanding have been identified by researchers as a potentially key instrument that can lower anti-social behavior and enhance positive social and educational outcomes.[149] In order to highlight this, Miller and colleagues[150] found that children who had more names for emotions and recognized emotions more accurately enjoyed higher levels of popularity among peers. As a result of this, it is important to have conversations with your child about all the different emotions and explore why people feel them in different situations.

INDEPENDENCE BUILDING

Today, I will identify my child's behavior, needs and emotions

WHAT DO I NEED TO DO?

We all display a range of behaviors every day and indeed we all witness our children displaying a variety of behaviors. The difference between our own behaviors and those of our children is that we understand why we are acting in a particular way but we are not always privy to this knowledge about our children. This task requires you to focus on what your child's behavior is telling you. Parents often focus on trying to promote positive behaviors and stop or prevent negative behaviors but today you are required to shift this focus down a more exploratory avenue. When your child displays any type of behavior, ask yourself why? This is not making excuses for behavior, rather, it is trying to discover what lies beneath any given behavior. It is about gaining practical experience in doing something that psychologists do all the time: reveal the need that is being identified by the behavior and then try to discover what feelings are occurring in the need.

WHY AM I DOING THIS?

Being able to manage a child's behaviors is a fundamental parenting skill. If children are left in a state of being unable to manage their behaviors, this can become rather disabling for the child as it may interfere with daily tasks and with how others perceive them. However, mostly, children are simply not able to manage their behaviors. The reason for this is, in order to truly manage behavior, the needs that are causing the behavior must first be met. It can be helpful to think of behaviors as an iceberg, whereby the behavior is the section visible to the world and the part below the water is the need. The feelings comprise the majority of the iceberg hidden under the surface of the sea. In managing behaviors, by identifying with the underlying needs and emotions, you are teaching your child about understanding themselves and others.[151] Research has shown that children whose parents help them to identify and cope with their experiences of negative emotions in a sympathetic and problem-solving oriented way are more likely to be friendlier and more empathetic towards others.[152,153]

#worriesawayday

Today, I will help my child to blow their worries away

#worriesawayday

WHAT DO I NEED TO DO?

Today, you want to help your child blow their worries away! To do this, you will need a stone, something that you can let blow into the air and something that you can write or draw with. You could use a balloon, a kite, a sky lantern, a feather, or any item that you feel is suitable. Explain to your child that they will be letting go of something that is worrying them today. You can explain this to them by drawing a worry of your own on to a stone and, then, show your child how carrying this stone around every day is a struggle, the same as carrying a worry around. Explain that today you are going to free yourselves from this 'worry-weight' by setting the worry free. You will first help your child identify what their worry-weight may be and, then, you will help them to write or draw their worry on to the item that they will set free. You will go somewhere suitable with your child for them to send their worry back into the universe, leaving them feeling lighter and free of the worry.

WHY AM I DOING THIS?

The most important thing you are doing today is helping your child find a way to identify and communicate something this is causing them to worry. Also, you are helping your child understand exactly what a worry is and the way that worries can impact on how we are feeling. Children can struggle with thinking abstractly about such things as feelings, thoughts and worries, so helping your child bring these abstract concepts into a place of concrete being will help the child to see them as tangible and manageable. It is very difficult to cope with something that you cannot make sense of, so today you are helping your child to understand their worries and resultant feelings. Following on from this, you are helping them to feel in control of these feelings by going through the process of expressing and dispensing of them. Research has found that simply putting words on feelings activates the prefrontal region of the brain and results in a reduced response in the amygdala. This basically means that the placement of a word on to a feeling will reduce one's emotional responses to the feeling, thus, resulting in the feeling having a less harmful impact on well-being.[154]

ACTIVITY-BASED LEARNING

#jarofwishes

Create a jar of family wishes

#jarofwishes

WHAT DO I NEED TO DO?

Today, set up a family wish jar. You can do this as a once-off activity and only need a small jar, or you can make this jar a permanent fixture in your house, which may require a larger one. Once you have your jar selected, you might like to get younger members of the family to decorate it. Tonight, before bedtime, ask each child to write/draw/color a wish that they have for their family and to place it in the jar. At the same time, write your own wish and add it to the jar too. If any family member is arriving home later, then they must add their wish upon departure for bed too. You might like to have a look at these wishes or you might not; you might like to add a wish daily or weekly or you might not; you might like to grant one of the wishes or you might not. Whatever you do from here is entirely up to you. For today, the important part is having each member of your family take a moment to think, not only about themselves, but about themselves in the context of their family unit and having this thought placed in the real world in a jar of wishes.

WHY AM I DOING THIS?

One element to working on a family bond is to work on individual's thoughts and that is what you are doing today. You are altering your family members' thought patterns by interrupting their usual pattern and asking them to think about what they wish for, for their family. This helps each family member to reframe their thoughts about themselves in the context of the family and, thus, reinforces their sense of belonging to the family. Having each family member write down their wishes not only gives you the option of having an insight into their hopes for your family and their present priorities, but the actual process of writing down these wishes has been proven to significantly benefit one's own sense of well-being. Additionally, the benefits of writing down emotions are evidenced by research, which shows that spending time writing about your best possible future attributes or about personal traumatic experiences is associated with increased health benefits, even up to five months after the practice of writing.[155]

FAMILY ATTACHMENT AND BONDING

#afeelingsgame

Make 'Feelings Eggs' with your child to build upon their ability to put names on to their feelings

#afeelingsgame

WHAT DO I NEED TO DO?

The main aim of today is to help your child put words on their feelings, which is something children of all ages struggle with. A good way to show your child how to identify their feelings is to make it into a game. There are many different feelings games that you can play and most are enjoyable to children of all ages. Making 'Feelings Eggs' is a simple game and, in order to do this, you need eggs which can be egg-shaped pieces of plastic or wood, or you can make them yourself from plaster or clay. You must be able to draw on the material that you make the egg shape from. With your children, try to think of as many types of feelings as possible and ask your child to describe and act out how they look when they are feeling each way. You and your child then draw this depiction of the feeling on to the egg. You can then choose a name for each egg incorporating the feeling word, for example, Happy Harry, Worry William, Sadness Sophie, and so on. Allow each child to contribute to shaping how the egg looks, choosing what colors suit the feeling, the type of face to draw on the egg and the hairstyle of the egg. Once you have your eggs made, you can sort them into egg boxes, keeping all the positive feelings together and all the negative feelings together! You can play any amount of games with your eggs after this to expose your children to a range of feelings and associated names.

WHY AM I DOING THIS?

The psychological term used for the ability to translate feelings into words is 'affect labelling' and this process is known to be one of the best ways to help people manage negative emotional experiences. So, by engaging in this simple activity that will expose your child to feelings words, you are equipping your children with a tool that will help them manage negative emotional experiences that may come their way. Evidence for this technique comes from studies that have demonstrated how verbally processing an emotional experience will produce less activity in the area of the brain responsible for emotional regulation, called the amygdala, than processing the experience mentally without verbalization.[154] This means that verbalizing helps the child process their feelings easily and more effectively.

INDEPENDENCE BUILDING

#kidsday90

#advicefreeday

Empower to learn by withdrawing from providing advice

#advicefreeday

WHAT DO I NEED TO DO?

Today, you are asked to take a step back from your role in advice-giving. You might be a parent who dishes out advice more frequently that hot dinners or you might be the type of parent who holds gems of advice for when they are really needed. Either way, for today, hold back and refrain from giving advice. Instead, when you child comes to you, help them to explore the issue until they arrive at their own solution. By doing this, you are helping your children learn, for themselves, about what is right and wrong. When your child approaches you today with a problem, first of all, praise them for coming to you so as they feel you are there as a decision-making support. Next, help them to digest the issue and explore all that it involves. At this point, you are not looking for a solution but are exploring the issue itself. Once an understanding of the issue is acquired by your child, you can move to assisting in the decision-making process. You do this by looking at options your child suggests and helping your child to evaluate these in terms of right and wrong, consequences for themselves, and the impact on others.

WHY AM I DOING THIS?

When we provide our child with advice on a situation, no matter how big or small, what we are really doing is letting the child know what our own life experiences have taught us. Providing advice is somewhat like providing the answers to a test; the child bypasses learning as they already have the solution. Of course, rearing a self-thinking child is about more than simply not giving advice but, by doing so, you are placed in a position where you need to learn an alternative approach to helping with your child's conundrums. For a long time, research has shown that a child will internalize moral principles when a parent takes the time to discuss with them how their actions will impact upon others.[156] More recent research has shown that, by adopting an authoritative parenting style (an approach that involves parents providing their children with explanations and moral consequences as opposed to strict rules and punishments), children are more likely to develop an internal moral understanding of right and wrong.[157]

FUNDAMENTAL PARENTING SKILL

#growyourwishes

Grow your wishes

#growyourwishes

WHAT DO I NEED TO DO?

Make something grow! Choose a plant, flowers, food, grass, a tree – anything that you can watch grow. Help your child to plant the seeds in a pot or in the garden and encourage them to be as involved in the process as possible – feeling the soil, digging, pouring, placing the seeds and patting it down. At the final phase of the planting, invite your child to plant their wishes with it so they can watch their wishes grow. Every day, encourage your child to water the plant to help their wishes grow. Inform them that plants like to be talked to in order to help them grow. This provides your child with an opportunity to talk to the plant about the wishes they are growing.

WHY AM I DOING THIS?

In addition to this being an activity that fosters opportunities for parental bonding, interaction with siblings, messy play, appreciation for nature, learning about natural growth, and a sense of responsibility, it also has the potential to offer deeper psychological benefits. There is a body of research that supports the power of positive affect, whereby being positive attracts further positivity. By your child spending time each day thinking about their positive wish, talking to their plant about their wish and nurturing their wish, they are being placed into a positive place where they are more likely to attract further positivity. Studies show that happy individuals are successful across multiple life domains, including relationships, friendships, and health. It is suggested that this is not simply because being successful makes one happy, but rather because positive affect leads to success.[158]

ACTIVITY-BASED LEARNING

#blendedstory

Today, my child and I will create a blended story

#blendedstory

WHAT DO I NEED TO DO?

The activity today involves nothing more than a pen, some paper and a few active imaginations. First, make sure you and your child are comfortable, free from distraction and are ready for some creativity. You write the first line of your story, for example, 'The girl could not believe what she had overheard on the bus' or 'The warm cozy hut looked beautiful covered in snow'. Your child will then be asked to tell you the next sentence of the story and you write it down. If there is more than one child, the process simply continues around in a circle until it is your time again. The story can naturally end when you both – or all as a group – feel it has concluded and there is no more to tell. Creative prompts may include talking about how the character felt, what the scene looked and smelled like, what the food tasted like, and what the animals sounded like.

WHY AM I DOING THIS?

The parent is the primary teacher in a child's life; you are the educator who teaches your child to speak, walk and have good manners. However, in order to enjoy a dynamic bond with your child, it is also important to experience your relationship in a different way as teaching reflects an imbalanced power relationship between 'teacher' and 'student'. This type of relationship suggests that the two individuals are different from one another, one of whom possesses mastery and domination.[159] However, by working in conjunction with one another on a creative project such as writing a story, we blur this distinct imbalance. This leads both/all parties to realize a connection between one another and eradicates the dominance of the parent-teacher over the child.[160,161] What happens is that you and your child view one another as equals, who are both working together as a team. As such, co-operation, idea-sharing and mutual regard are promoted and enhanced during this activity.

FAMILY ATTACHMENT AND BONDING

#allpermissionsgranted

Grant your child a solid 'YES' to all permissions requested today, so long as it is safe to do so, of course!

#allpermissionsgranted

WHAT DO I NEED TO DO?

Sometimes children become over-reliant on asking for permission to do things and it can limit their own decision-making process. As such, today you are going to take yourself out of the permission-granting equation by consistently answering with a solid 'YES'. Of course, this needs to be done within reasonable limits and you are not to grant permission to something unreasonable or dangerous. It is useful to limit yourself to granting permission to things that apply to the moment, for example, 'Mam, can I have a yogurt?' or 'Dad, can I have go upstairs to play?' Basically, when at all possible, say "Yes"! There are some creative ways that you can incorporate 'Yes' into your response, without giving full permission per se. You can acquiesce but add limits to your 'Yes', for instance, by limiting the amount of time or money spent. You can agree but attach responsibilities, for instance, by adding what needs to be done to ensure responsible practices. For example, 'Yes, you can borrow the car but you need to stay below the speed limit.' You can say 'Yes' but suggest an alternative time, for instance, 'Yes we can play a game together but we will have our dinner first and then the game.' You can agree, but help your child to examine its reasonableness. For instance, if they are asking for their third yogurt, you can say 'Yes' but ask them to first decide if it is fair that there would be no yogurts left for tomorrow.

WHY AM I DOING THIS?

Most children are familiar with hearing 'No', and the impact of this can diminish away. By using 'Yes' as often as you can, you are actually empowering your 'No' because children attend more to language they are less familiar with. Additionally, a child's spirit will be raised significantly when they find you agreeing with them more often as it reaffirms their independent thought processes. By granting your child permission regularly, you are letting your child know that you are both equals, thus, further empowering them to be independent decision-makers.[162] Research suggests that, when parents attend to and accept their children's goals, they are more likely to create a supportive environment for their children to learn important developmental skills which will help them manage challenges into adulthood.[163]

INDEPENDENCE BUILDINC

#kidsday94

#today4tomorrow

Today, my child and I will build a time-capsule for tomorrow

#today4tomorrow

WHAT DO I NEED TO DO?

Thinking about the fact that who you are today will impact upon who you are tomorrow is a difficult thing for people of all ages to understand. This is particularly salient for children as they are not always sure about who they really are as their identity is an ever-changing state. Today, you will help your child form an understanding of who they are at this moment in time. You will do this by helping each child to make their own time-capsule containing items that will help their future selves understand and learn from their present selves. Help your child to find things that represent aspects of their personality and how they see themselves in their world today. In doing this, the children can write notes, draw pictures, select stones or shells, include colors to show their feelings, select pictures to show the people in their lives, use birthday cards, memories from days out, or family trees. Your child might like to do a 'Me Map', where they place others in relation to themselves on a map like you can find in the resource section of your members area of www.100happydays4kids.com. What each child wants to include is up to them but, before they bury the capsule, encourage each child to write a note or draw a picture for their future selves, sharing all the things they hope to become as they grow up. Once complete, help your child to find a safe spot to bury their time-capsule and to mark it for when their future selves come a-digging!

WHY AM I DOING THIS?

There are a huge number of benefits to creating a time-capsule. The process itself is one that brings an opportunity to engage in a shared activity with others, thus, enhancing bonding. It encourages children to talk about their experiences and about themselves which is highly therapeutic in itself. It helps children to practice their reflection skills and their goal-setting abilities. This process involves an element of self-inquiry, which can help a child develop an understanding of who they are in the context of their world, thus, enhancing their development of Theory of Mind. This activity can enhance the development of a child's social understanding also, which has been shown to occur through the communicative interaction of the child's experience of the world with others.

ACTIVITY-BASED LEARNING

#kidsday95

#familyshowoff

Take your family out and show them off

#familyshowoff

WHAT DO I NEED TO DO?

So you love your family, right? Well, most of the time anyway! Today, your task is to show off this wonderful family of yours to the world. Many families spend so much time in their houses or driving kids from one activity to the next but today, leave your worries at home and take your family out to embrace the world. Go out with no agenda other than to enjoy each other's company and show the world how you appreciate each other. Where you go and what you do is entirely up to you - the important thing is that you are able to exist as a loving family unit out in the public domain. Hold hands, exchange kisses, skip along, laugh out loud, watch and listen to each other, make the world your world for today and enjoy every minute of it.

WHY AM I DOING THIS?

What you are doing today is working on your family's collective social identity. In addition to internal identities, people also have external identities, referred to as one's public image. For children, there is often a conflict between how they see themselves and how others see them, resulting in the child making a conscious effort to work on portraying a public image that they feel is attractive to others.[164] Today, by being a happy family engaging in positive interactions out in the world, you are providing your children with a social support that they can use as a safety net when they are easing the conflict between their public image and their self-identity. Research shows that social well-being is positively related to the expression of positive emotion, regulation of negative emotions and open communication with parents.[165]

#mycommunity

Today, I will help my child identify with their community

#checkingin

WHAT DO I NEED TO DO?

Start by exploring your child's concept of their community by crafting a physical community model, drawing one or writing about their community. You will need to help your child to look at all the different categories that make up a community from the buildings, services and resources to the teams, people, and personalities. Next, help your child to identify your family's role in the community and then their own individual role. They can do this by writing or drawing their family members into the community picture and then placing themselves wherever they want. Once your child has a sense of community spirit, guide them towards deciding how they could be more involved with their community or how they could adopt a different role within their community in line with their own interests and needs.

WHY AM I DOING THIS?

By facilitating your child's exploration of their community and their roles within their community, you are helping with your child's development of their sense of self. Who one is in relation to their community is an important part of understanding one's self-concept. Evidence indicates that engaging in a community-based activity can improve one's self confidence, help children deal with a range of challenges, provide them with the experience of communicating with a variety of people, and builds up important life skills, all within a supportive environment. Additionally, having something meaningful that gets children and families involved will have a positive effect on overall mood, bring about a feeling of belonging and having a purpose outside of the home, all of which can help prevent the onset of sadness and depression.[166]

INDEPENDENCE BUILDING

#kidsday97

#fourseasonswinter

Four seasons – Winter

#fourseasonswinter

Today is the fourth and final day that we will experience Vivaldi's Four Seasons with our child, which means we will listen to the full concerto of Winter and you are asked to sit close to your child, while you both work on your separate pieces of art. Your child now has had some experience with learning how to listen to music, synchronize this with their imagination and put it down on paper. However, we also want for your child to feel comfortable doing this with their parent working independently alongside them. Afterwards, you are asked to hang your child's four masterpieces up on a wall and talk to them about whether they LOOK like the four different seasons. It might be fun to have other members of your family or close friends to guess which pictures they think represent which seasons.

WHY AM I DOING THIS?

Aside from the relaxing effects of this music that we have outlined in previous Vivaldi tasks, you and your child will benefit from the artful expression of this last concerto. Producing a visual reaction to this cultural piece of music is incredibly insightful as it enhances a sense of ownership of the art, which reinforces powerful connections between their learning and private passions.[167] Hanging these four masterpieces on the wall, if your child agrees, allows for them to know that their expressions and opinions are an integral part of their home and are valued by every member. Receiving positive feedback results in the child feeling proud, encouraged and enthused about what they have done. Finally, the pieces on the wall serve as a constant reminder of their achievement and may inspire them to produce more art which combines the auditory, imaginative and visual interplay of creativity.

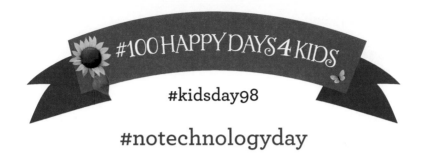

Today, my family will take a break from technology

#notechnologyday

WHAT DO I NEED TO DO?

The task today will benefit both parents and children, but you may find it more difficult than previous tasks. In this age of modern technology, we are constantly being bombarded from all angles by technology. It would be difficult to imagine how to adapt if technology was to suddenly disappear. Today, the aim is for all the family to NOT use technology and focus instead on old-fashioned entertainments, such as chatting, board-games and baking together. If this seems a little too difficult, why not attempt a ban on technology for as long as possible. Perhaps, you could manage six hours? The aim is to recognize how distracting these devices can be and also how much time we really spend attending to our technological accessories.

WHY AM I DOING THIS?

Children in modern times are often experts at using technology, especially with the recent portability of devices, including smart phones and tablets[168] although, the overuse of computers has been problematic for many years.[169] One of the most important and common concerns for developmental psychologists includes internet addiction, defined as "an individual's inability to control their internet use, which in turn leads to feelings of distress, functional impairment of daily activities, and denial of the problematic behaviours".[170] Unfortunately, there are many other detrimental effects attached to the over-use of technology, including negative effects on the development of physical, psychological, and social abilities.[171] Researchers have also found that engaging in activities utilizing technology increases children's risk of developing addictive disorders, depression, aggressiveness and desensitization to suffering, and that this may blur the child's ability to distinguish the real world from fantasy or simulation.[172]

#ourfamilydecision

Involve your children in making a decision that is important for your family

#ourfamilydecision

You first need to decide what family issue you need to resolve, which can be big or small. You must all make this family decision together and nothing will be final until you have found something that you can all agree upon. You will start by letting the children know what it is that needs to be decided upon and then give the open floor to each member to hear their initial thoughts. The next stage is to explore options, which involves you outlining a few alternatives that are based on all of your initial thoughts and explore these options individually whilst remaining open to incorporating any newly emerging suggestions. You will continue to work through these options until you arrive at one that is agreeable to everyone.

WHY AM I DOING THIS?

Having children involved in a decision-making process gives them greater insight into the process and a fuller understanding about why things are changing. Additionally, it provides children with the opportunity to see how an outcome they have contributed to and agreed upon may turn out to have very different consequences than initially expected and, thus, may need to be revisited. Research has shown that being able to exercise choice is a positively valuable experience.[173] Studies have shown that parents can actively nurture empowerment in their children by displaying encouragement and trust, having high expectations of them, and providing them with support regardless of the outcomes of their decisions.[174]

INDEPENDENCE BUILDING

#100 HAPPY DAYS 4 KIDS

#kidsday100

#wowyoumadeit

Wow, you made it!

THANK YOU!

Thank you so much for joining us on this wonderful journey across a terrain of learning, exploration and adventure. We hope that you have discovered a host of new treasures about yourself, your child and your family. For us, our main aim is to change how parents view their children, such that they can be more mindful about who this little person is and what small changes can be made to make them have happier days. They are active little beings, who are learning hundreds of new concepts, perspectives and facts every single day and deserve the same respect, encouragement and assistance as adults do, if not more. We hope you have learned how beneficial it is to listen to your child, give them their space, value their opinion, promote their independence, celebrate their uniqueness and cherish their being a part of your life.

As co-authors, we would like to thank you for taking the time to follow us through one hundred activities, which we hope have assisted you to become a better parent. It has been an overwhelmingly delightful experience creating a piece of work, which has the potential to make such an important impact on so many families' lives around the world. Remember to use as many of these skills as you can into the future and never give up on being a positive influence on your child – it will be worth it! You can always use this book again to reference back to tasks you think might be beneficial when your child is older. For now, take some time to look back over your journey and reflect on your family's happiness.

With a happier generation growing up, we can contribute to a happier world!

Love and peace,

Arlene M. Naughten
BA, PGCertPBPT, PGDipPsych,
PGDipEd, MScPsych, MScFPsychC

Lorraine M. Lynch
BA, PGDipPsych, MScHPsych,
PhD Researcher

About the authors

ARLENE M. NAUGHTEN

Arlene Naughten is the Founder and Clinical Director of Sugru – Child Development & Contextual Therapy Services, where she offers professional services to suit the developmental and therapeutic needs of children and families.

Arlene graduated from National University of Ireland, Galway with a Bachelor of Arts in Psychological Studies and Philosophy, a Postgraduate Diploma in Education, and a Postgraduate Certificate in Therapeutic Play, as accredited by the Academy of Play and Child Psychotherapy. Arlene achieved a Postgraduate Diploma in Psychology from Royal Holloway, University of London; a Master of Science in Psychology and a Master of Science in Forensic Psychology and Criminology from The Open University. Presently, Arlene is continuing her professional development on the Doctoral Programme of Psychology with Middlesex University London.

In her years of practice, Arlene has completed Continual Professional Development training in a broad range of areas including child protection, domestic violence, mindfulness, family therapy, missing people, suicide prevention, sexual right, intellectual disabilities, and TEFL.

#100HappyDays4Kids was the winner of the SCCUL ONE TO WATCH Award 2014

Arlene holds memberships with the Teaching Council of Ireland, the Psychological Society of Ireland, the British Psychological Society, and Play Therapy Ireland; of which Arlene is led by the codes of ethical practice of these professional bodies. Arlene is a member of the Accredited Voluntary Register, Register of Play Therapy and Creative Arts Therapists which is regulated by the UK's Professional Standards Authority.

Arlene currently lectures part-time with Athlone Institute of Technology and has a range of experience lecturing in the topics of Child Protection, Law, Education, Psychology, Child Development, and Parenting.

For many years, Arlene has worked providing a range of therapeutic and support services for people with intellectual disabilities, mental health difficulties, and neurodevelopmental disorders; and with children, parents, and families dealing with a variety of issues such as domestic violence, child abuse, child neglect, self harm, suicidal ideation, trafficking, issues in foster care, and attachment issues, to include but a few.

This is Arlene's first book, however she has acted as contributing author on other publications in the field and has written a range of mindfulness, child development, and parenting programmes.

Currently, Lorraine Lynch is a Doctoral Research Fellow in the University of Limerick, conducting interdisciplinary research on Dyspraxia with the Psychology and the Physical Education and Social Sciences (PESS) departments. She also holds the position of Head of Research with Sugru, a child development and contextualized play therapy center based in Ireland, where she specializes in work with children with neurodevelopmental disorders and their families.

Lorraine graduated from the National University of Ireland, Galway with a Bachelor of Arts in English and Psychological Science. Following from this, Lorraine achieved a Postgraduate Diploma in Psychology from the Open University and First-Class Honours in a Master of Science in Health Psychology from the University of Ulster, including a Class-A Distinction in her dissertation.

She has completed Continual Professional Development courses in the use of a number of intervention strategies, research software, suicide prevention, child protection, mindfulness, therapeutic play, mental health advocacy, neurodevelopmental conditions, and TEFL.

Lorraine is registered with the Psychological Society of Ireland and the British Psychological Society and adheres to the strict codes of practices of the aforementioned professional entities.

She has extensive experience working with children and families presenting with a variety of needs within the realm of health psychology, including well-being, chid protection, addiction and mental health difficulties.

Lorraine has worked with children with mild to severe developmental delays, as well as with children requiring therapeutic intervention in Ireland, America, Africa and Asia.

She is affiliated with the Dyspraxia Association of Ireland through research and practice. Lorraine's primary role is in forging new ways of assisting those with neurodevelopmental disorders using a holistic approach through social support and individualized therapeutic programmes.

LORRAINE M. LYNCH

Bibliography

1   Clarke, A. (2004). *Listening as a way of life: Why and how we listen to young children.* National Children's Bureau.

2   Tolfree, D. & Woodhead, M. (1999). Tapping a Key Resource. *Early Childhood Matters, 91,* 19-23.

3   Lieberman, M.D, Eisenberger, N. I., Crockett, M. J., Tom, S., Pfeifer, J. H. & Way, B. M. (2007). Putting feelings into words affect labelling disrupts amygdala activity in response to affective stimuli. *Psychological Science, 18(5),* 421-8.

4   Wiltermuth, S. S. & Heath, C. (2009). Synchrony and Cooperation. *Psychological Science, 20(1),* 1-5.

5   Kabat-Zinn, J. (2003). Mindfulness-based interventions in context: Past, present, and future. *Clinical Psychology: Science and Practice, 10,* 144-56.

6   Snow, C. E. & Beals, D. E. (2006), Mealtime talk that supports literacy development. *New Directions for Child and Adolescent Development,* 51-66.

7   Hofferth, S. L. & Sandberg, J. F. (2001). How American Children Spend Their Time. *Journal of Marriage and Family, 63,* 295-308.

8   Eisenberg , M. E., Olson, R. E., Neumark-Sztainer, D., Story, M., & Bearinger, L. H. (2004). Correlations Between Family Meals and Psychosocial Well-being Among Adolescents. *Arch Paediatric Adolescence Medical Journal, 158(8),* 792-6.

9   Utter, J., Denny, S., Robinson, E., Fleming, T., Ameratunga, S. & Grant, S. (2013). Family meals and the well-being of adolescents. *Journal of Pediatrics and Child Health, 49,* 906-11.

10 Fulkerson, J. A., Story, M., Mellin, A., Leffert, N., Neumark-Sztainer, D. & French, S. A. (2005). Family Dinner Meal Frequency and Adolescent Development: Relationships with Developmental Assets and High-Risk Behaviours. *Journal of Adolescent Health, 39(3),* 337-45.

11 Welsh, E. M., French, S. A., & Wall, M. (2011). Examining the Relationship Between Family Meal Frequency and Individual Dietary Intake: Does Family Cohesion Play a Role? *Journal of Nutrition Education and Behavior, 43(4),* 229-35.

12 Field, T. M., Woodson, R., Greenberg, R. & Cohen, D. (1982). Discrimination and imitation of facial expressions by neonates. *Science, 218,* 179-81.

13 Meltzoff, A. N. & Moore, M. K. (1988). *The origins of imitation in infancy: Paradigm, phenomena, and theories.* In C. Rovee-Colier, & L. P. Lipsitt (Eds.), *Advances in infancy research.* Norwood, NJ: Ablex.

14 Wörmann, V., Holodynski, M., Kärtner, J. & Keller, H. (2012). A cross-cultural comparison of the development of the social smile: A longitudinal study of maternal and infant imitation in 6- and 12-week-old infants. *Infant Behavior & Development, 35(3),* 335-47.

15 Teichmann, H., Göllnitz, G., & Göhler, I. (1975). The origin and effects on schoolchildren of high parental demands for achievement. *International Journal Of Mental Health, 4(4),* 83-106.

16   Cervellin, G. & Lippi, G. (2011). From music-beat to heart-beat: a journey in the complex interactions between music, brain and heart. *European Journal of International Medicine, 22,* 371-4.

17   Gooding, L., Swezey, S. & Zwischenberger, J. B. (2012). Using music interventions in perioperative care. *South Medical Journal, 105,* 486-90.

18   Koelsch, S. & Siebel, W. A. (2005). Towards a neural basis of music perception. *Trends in Cognitive Science, 9,* 578-84.

19   Pérez-Lloret, S., Diez, J., Domé, M. N., Alvarez Delvenne, A., Braidot, N., Cardinali, D. P. & Vigo, D. E. (2014). Effects of different "relaxing" music styles on the autonomic nervous system. *Noise & Health, 16,* 279-84.

20   Sliwka, A., Nowobilski, R., Polczyk, R., Nizankowska-Mogilnicka, E. & Szczeklik, A. (2012). Mild asthmatics benefit from music therapy. *Journal of Asthma, 49,* 401-8.

21   Axline, V. (1947). *Play therapy.* New York, NY: Ballantine Books.

22   Bratton, S., Ray, D., Rhine, T. & Jones, L. (2005). The efficacy of play therapy with children: A meta-analytic review of treatment outcomes. *Professional Psychology: Research and Practice, 36,* 376-90.

23   Greeno, J. G. (1998). The situativity of knowing, learning, and research. *American Psychologist, 53,* 5-26.

24   Walsh, F. (2003). Family resilience: a framework for clinical practice. *Family Processes, 42,* 1-18.

25   Eckhoff, A. (2006). Influences on children's aesthetic responses: The role of prior knowledge, contexts, and social experiences during interactions with the visual arts. Unpublished doctoral dissertation, University of Colorado, Boulder, CO. Cited in: Eckhoff, A. (2013). Conversational Pedagogy: Exploring Interactions Between a Teaching Artist and Young Learners During Visual Arts Experiences. *Early Childhood Education Journal, 41(5),* 365-72.

26   Hetland, L., Winner, E., Veenema, S. & Sheridan, K. (2007). *Studio thinking: The real benefits of visual arts education.* New York, NY: Teachers College Press.

27   Schirrmacher, R. (2002). *Arts and creative development for young children* (4th ed.) New York, NY: Delmer Press.

28   Striker, S. (2001). *Young at art: Teaching toddlers self-expression, problem solving skills and an appreciation for art.* New York, NY: Henry Holt. Cited in: Eckhoff, A. (2013). Conversational Pedagogy: Exploring Interactions Between a Teaching Artist and Young Learners During Visual Arts Experiences. *Early Childhood Education Journal, 41(5),* 365-72.

29   Larson, M. C., White, B. P., Cochran, A., Donzella, B. & Gunnar, M. (1998). Dampening of the cortisol response to handling at 3 months in human infants and its relation to sleep, circadian cortisol activity, and behavioral distress. *Developmental Psychobiology, 33,* 327-37.

30   Mindell, J.A., Kuhn, B., Lewin, D.S., Meltzer, L.J. & Sadeh, A. (2006). Behavioral treatment of bedtime problems and night wakings in infants and young children. *Sleep, 29*(10), 1263-76.

31   Bandura, A. (1977). *Social Learning Theory.* Englewood Cliffs, NJ: Prentice Hall.

32   Cummings, E. M. & Davies, P. T. (1996). Emotional security as a regulatory process in normal development and the development of psychopathology. *Development and Psychopathology, 8,* 123-39.

33 Eisenberg, N., Zhou, Q., Spinrad, T. L., Valiente, C., Fabes, R. A. & Liew, J. (2005). Relations among positive parenting, children's effortful control, and externalizing problems: a three-wave longitudinal study.

34 Cimprich, B. & Ronis, D. (2003). An environmental intervention to restore attention in women with newly diagnosed breast cancer. *Cancer Nursing, 26*(4), 284-91.

35 Ogunseitan, O. (2005). Topophilia and the quality of life. *Environmental Health Perspectives 113 (2),* 143-8.

36 Pretty, J., Peacock, J., Sellens, M. & Griffin, M. (2005). The mental and physical health outcomes of green exercise. *International Journal of Environmental Health Research 15(5),* 319-37.

37 Stern, P.C. (2000). Toward a coherent theory of environmentally significant behavior. *Journal of Social Issues, (56)*, 407-24

38 Zisapel, N. (2007). Sleep and sleep disturbances: Biological basis and clinical implications. *Cellular and Molecular Life Sciences, 64(10),* 1174-86.

39 Larson, R. W. (Ed), Wiley, A. R. (Ed) & Branscomb, K. R. (Ed) (2006). *Family mealtime as a context of development and socialization,* Jossey-Bass: San Francisco.

40 Nordquest, M. A. & Nordquest, M. (2007). Review of 'Family mealtime as a context of development and socialization'. *Families, Systems, & Health, 25(2),* 219-21.

41 Burnett, P. C. (1999). Children's Self-Talk and Academic Self-Concepts. *Educational Psychology in Practice,15*(3), 195.

42 Philpot, V. D., Holliman, W. B. & Madonna, S. (1995). Self-statements, locus of control, and depression in predicting self-esteem. *Psychological Reports, 76,* 1007-10.

43 Percy, M. S. (2010). Feeling loved, having friends to count on, and taking care of myself: Minority children living in poverty describe what is "special" to them. *Journal of Children and Poverty, 9(1),* 55-70.

44 Reidun, U. (2002). Serotonin and sleep. *Sleep Medicine Reviews, 6(1),* 55–67.

45 Glasser, H. (2013). Exploring the Nurtured Heart online course. Retrieved from http://www.childrenssuccessfoundation.com/nhatrainings/.

46 Benson, H. & Proctor, W. (2010). *Relaxation Revolution: Enhancing Your Personal Health Through the Science and Genetics of Mind Body Healing*. UK: Simon & Schuster.

47 Figer, R. C. (2008). Looking Through the Eyes of the Child: The Phenomenon of Child Verbal Abuse in the Philippines. *Relational Child & Youth Care Practice,21*(4), 46-58.

48 Willoughby, B. B., Richard, R. B., Jennifer, C. C., Brant, P. H., Tucker, B. & Shauna, L. S. *(2010). Substance Abuse Special Issue: Mindfulness-Related Treatments and Addiction Recovery, 31(2),* 86-97.

49 Anderson, D., Piscitelli, B., Weier, K., Everett, M. & Tayler, C. (2002), Children's Museum Experiences: Identifying Powerful Mediators of Learning. *Curator: The Museum Journal, 45,* 213-31.

50 Brown, J. D. & Siegel, J.M. (1988). Exercise as a buffer of life stress: A prospective study of adolescent health. *Health Psychology, 7(4),* 341-53.

51 Moore, E. R., Anderson, G. C., Bergman, N. & Dowswell, T. (2012). Early skin-to-skin contact for mothers and their healthy newborn infants. *The Cochrane Collaboration.*

52 Uvnas-Moberg, K. (1998). Oxytocin may mediate the benefits of positive social interactions and emotions. *Psychoneuroendocrinology, 23(8),* 19-35.

53 Warneken, F. & Tomasello, M. (2006). Altruistic helping in human infants and young chimpanzees. *Science, 311,* 1301-3.

54 Warneken, F. & Tomasello, M. (2008). Extrinsic rewards undermine altruistic tendencies in 20-month-olds. *Developmental Psychology, 44,* 1785-8.

55 Warneken, F. & Tomasello, M. (2009). The roots of human altruism. *British Journal of Psychology, 100,* 455-71.

56 Piliavin, J. A. (2009). Altruism and helping: The evolution of a field: The 2008 Cooley-Mead Presentation. *Social Psychology Quarterly, 72,* 209-25.

57 Ongley, S. F., Nola, M., Malti, T., Sommerville, J. & Kienbaum, J. (2014). Children's giving: moral reasoning and moral emotions in the development of donation behaviors. *Frontiers in Psychology,* 51-8.

58 Knafo, A. & Plomin, R. (2006). Prosocial behaviour from early to middle childhood: genetic and environmental influences on stability and change. *Developmental Psychology, 42,* 771-86.

59 Staub, E. (1979). *Positive Social Behavior and Morality, Volume II: Socialization and Development.* New York: Academic Press.

60 Duffy, B. (1998). *Supporting Creativity and Imagination in the Early Years.* Milton Keynes: Open University Press.

61 Piaget, J. (1926). *The Languages and Thoughts of the Child.* London: Routledge and Kegan

62 Shaywitz, B. A. (2002). Disruption of posterior brain systems for reading in children with developmental dyslexia. *Biological Psychiatry, 52(2),* 101-10.

63 Rogoff, B. (1992). *Apprenticeship in Thinking: Cognitive Development in Social Context.* UK: Oxford University Press.

64 Bruner, J. (1996). *The Culture of Education.* Cambridge Mass: Harvard University Press.

65 Calkins, S. D. (1994). *Origins and outcomes of individual differences in emotion regulation.* In N. A. Fox (Ed.) The development of emotion regulation. Biological and behavioural considerations (*Monograph of the Society for Research in Child Development, 59,* 53–72.

66 Rydell, A., Thorell, L. B. & Bohlin, G. (2007). Emotion regulation in relation to social functioning: An investigation of child self-reports. *European Journal of Developmental Psychology, 4(3),* 293-313.

67 Burd, J., Weiner, M. & Tangorra, J. (2011). Look, listen, touch, feel, taste: The importance of sensory play. *Highscope Extensions, 25(5),* 2-5.

68 Higgins, T. E. (1981). *The "communication game": Implications for social cognition and persuasion.* In: E. T. Higgins, C. P. Herman & M. P Zanna. [eds.] (1981*) Social cognition: The Ontario symposium.* Hillsdale, NJ: Lawrence Erlbaum Associates.

69 United Nations (2010). The UN Convention on the Rights of the Child.

70   Gillespie, A.H. & Gillespie, G.W. (2007). Family food decision-making: an ecological systems framework. *Journal of Family Consumer Science. 99(2)*, 22-8.

71   Davies, P. T. & Cummings, E. M. (1994). Marital conflict and child adjustment: An emotional security hypothesis. *Psychological Bulletin, 116,* 387-411

72   Ginsburg, K. R. (2007). The Importance of Play in Promoting Healthy Child Development and Maintaining Strong Parent-Child Bonds. *American Academy of Paediatrics.*

73   Hurwitz, S. C. (2003). To be successful: let them play! *Child Education, 79,* 101-2.

74   Erickson, R. J. (1985). Play contributes to the full emotional development of the child. *Education, 105,* 261-3.

75   Pellegrini, A. D. & Smith, P. K. (1998). The development of play during childhood: forms and possible functions. *Child Psychology and Psychiatry Rev, 3,* 51-7.

76   Knight, N. K. (2013). Evaluating experience in funny ways: how friends bond through conversational hum. *Text & Talk, 33*(4/5), 553-74.

77   Dumas, J. E., Blechman, E. A. & Prinz, R. J. (1994). Aggressive Children and Effective Communication. *Aggressive Behavior, 20(5),* 347-58.

78   Kabat-Zinn, J. (2003). Mindfulness-based interventions in context: Past, present, and future. *Clinical Psychology: Science and Practice, 10,* 144-56.

79   Koelsch, S. & Siebel, W. A. (2005). Towards a neural basis of music perception. *Trends in Cognitive Science, 9,* 578-84.

80   Cervellin, G. & Lippi, G. (2011). From music-beat to heart-beat: a journey in the complex interactions between music, brain and heart. *European Journal of International Medicine, 22,* 371-4.

81   Sliwka, A., Nowobilski, R., Polczyk, R., Nizankowska-Mogilnicka, E. & Szczeklik, A. (2012). Mild asthmatics benefit from music therapy. *Journal of Asthma, 49,* 401-8.

82   Gooding, L., Swezey, S. & Zwischenberger, J. B. (2012). Using music interventions in perioperative care. *South Medical Journal, 105,* 486-90.

83   Pérez-Lloret, S., Diez, J., Domé, M. N., Alvarez Delvenne, A., Braidot, N., Cardinali, D. P. & Vigo, D. E. (2014). Effects of different "relaxing" music styles on the autonomic nervous system. *Noise & Health, 16,* 279-84.

84   Kornfield, J. (1977). *Living Buddhist masters.* Santa Cruz: Unity Press.

85   Blair, D. (2009). The child in the garden: An evaluative review of the benefits of school gardening. *Journal of Environmental Education, 40(2),* 15-38.

86   Fowler, J. H. & Chrisakis, N. A. (2010). Cooperative behavior cascades in human social networks. *National Academy of Sciences,* 107, 10.

87   Layous, K., Nelson, S. K., Oberle, E., Schonert-Reichl, K. A & Lyubomirsky, S. (2012). Kindness Counts: Prompting Prosocial Behavior in Preadolescents Boosts Peer Acceptance and Well-Being. 513-80.

88   Bergen, D. (2002). The role of pretend play in children's cognitive development. *Early Childhood Research and Practice, 4,* 1.

89   Starkweather, S. (2012). Telling family stories: collaborative storytelling, taking precedence and giving precedence in family group interviews with Americans in Singapore. *Area*, *44*(3), 289-95.

90   Erikson, E. (1967). *Childhood and Society.* Harmondsworth: Penguin.

91   Papadopoulou, M. (2012). The Ecology of Role Play: Intentionality and Cultural Evolution. *British Educational Research Journal, 38(4),* 575-92.

92   Fumikazu, F., Hidekazu, O., Yukiko, O., & Erika, T. (2014). The Effect of Other Children's Knowledge and Self Role-Taking on Preschoolers' Changing Their Explanation about Stories. *Japanese Journal of Developmental Psychology, 25(3),* 313-22.

93   Duff, S, E. (1996). A study of the effects of group family play on family relations. *International Journal of Play Therapy, 5(2),* 81-93.

94   Zabriskie, R. B. & McCormick, B. P. (2003). Parent and child perspectives of family leisure involvement and satisfaction with family life. *Journal of Leisure Research, 35(2),*163-89

95   Epstein, A. S. (2003). How Planning and Reflection Develop Young Children's Thinking Skills. *Journal of Young Children,* 28-36.

96   Harter, S. (1985). *The Self-Perception Profile for Children: Revision of the Perceived Competence Scale for Children.* University of Denver, Denver, CO.

97   Butler, R. J. & Gasson, S. L. (2005). Self esteem/self concept scales for children and adolescents: A review. *Child and Adolescent Mental Health, 10,* 190-201.

98   Brittain, W. L. (1979). *Creativity, Art, and the Young Child.* New York: Macmillan Publishing

99   Raeff, C. (2010). Independence and Interdependence in Children's Developmental Experiences. *Child Development Perspectives*, *4(1),* 31-6.

100 Wood, L. & Harper, C. (2008). The link between child nutrition and health: Overview of research in the UK. *Children's Food Trust.*

101 Carroll, J. B. (1963). A Model of School Learning. *Teachers College Record, 64(8),* 723-33.

102 Smith, C. & Carlson, B. E. (1997). Stress, Coping and Resilence in Children and Youth. *Social Service Review, 71(2),* 231-56.

103 Teichmann, H., Göllnitz, G. & Göhler, I. (1975). The origin and effects on schoolchildren of high parental demands for achievement. *International Journal of Mental Health*, 4(4), 83-106.

104 McMurray, R. G., Forsythe, W. A., Mar, M. H. & Hardy, C. J. (1987). Exercise intensity-related responses of beta-endorphin and catecholamines. *Medicine and Science in Sports and Exercise, 19(6),* 570-4.

105 Klein, S. A. & Deffenbacher, J. L. (1977). Relaxation and Exercise for Hyperactive Impulsive Children. *Perceptual and Motor Skills, 45(3),* 1159-62.

106 Han, K. (2007). Responses to six major terrestrial biomes in terms of scenic beauty, preference, and restorativeness. *Environment and Behavior, 39(4),* 529-56.

107 Erikson, E. (1967). *Childhood and Society.* Harmondsworth: Penguin.

108 Fish, M., Stifter, C.A. & Belsky, J. (1991). Conditions of continuity and discontinuity in infant negative emotionality: newborn to five months. *Child Development, 62,* 1525-37.

109 Hohmann, M. & Weikart, D. (1995). *Educating young children.* USA: The High/Scope Press.

110   Chen, L. H., Chen, M. Y. & Tsai, Y. M. (2012). Does gratitude always work? Ambivalence over emotional expression inhibits the beneficial effect of gratitude on well-being. *International Journal of Psychology, 47(5)*, 381-92.

111   Chen, L. H. & Kee, Y. H. (2008). Gratitude and adolescent athletes' well-being. *Social Indicators Research, 89(2)*, 361-73.

112   Froh, J. J., Charles, Y. & Todd, B. K. (2009). Gratitude and subjective well–being in early adolescence: Examining gender differences. *Journal of Adolescence, 32(3)*, 633-50.

113   Wood, A. M., Joseph, S. & Maltby, J. (2008). Gratitude uniquely predicts satisfaction with life: Incremental validity above the domains and facets of the five factor model. *Personality and Individual Differences, 45(1)*, 49-54.

114   Fredrickson, B. L. (2004). *Gratitude, like other positive emotion, broadens and builds.* In Emmons, R. A. & McCullough, M. E. (Eds.). *The psychology of gratitude.* New York, NY: Oxford University Press.

115   Larson, L. R., Green, G. T. & Cordell, H. K. (2011). Children's Time Outdoors: Results and Implications of the National Kids Survey. *Journal of Park & Recreation Administration*, *29*(2), 1-20.

116   Louv, R. (2008). *Last child in the woods: Saving our children from nature-deficit disorder.* Chapel Hill, NC: Algonquin Books of Chapel Hill.

117   Zaradic, P. A., & Pergams, O. R. W. (2007). Videophilia: Implications for childhood development and conservation. *Journal of Developmental Processes, 2*, 130-44.

118   Emmons, R. A. (2007). *Thanks: how the new science of gratitude can make you happier.* New York, NY: Houghton Mifflin Company. Cited in Chun, S. & Lee, Y. (2013). "I am just thankful": the experience of gratitude following traumatic spinal cord injury. *Disability & Rehabilitation, 35(1)*, 11-9.

119   Toussaint, L. & Friedman, P. (2009). Forgiveness, gratitude, and well-being: The mediating role of affect and beliefs. *Journal of Happiness Studies, 10,* 635-54.

120   Epstein, A.S. (2003). How Planning and Reflection Develop Young Children's Thinking Skills. *Journal of Young Children*, 28-36.

121   Cole, P. M. & Zahn-Waxler, C. (1994). Expressive control during a disappointment: Variations related to preschoolers' behavior problems. *Developmental Psychology*, *30(6)*, 835.

122   Erikson, E. (1967). *Childhood and Society.* Harmondsworth: Penguin.

123   Carlson, R. & Arthur, N. (1999). Play therapy and the therapeutic use of story. *Canada Journal of Counselling, 33(3)*, 212-26.

124   Raeff, C. (2010). Independence and Interdependence in Children's Developmental Experiences. *Child Development Perspectives*, *4(1)*, 31-6.

125   St George, J. M. & Fletcher, R. J. (2012). Time for work, commuting, and parenting? Commuting parents' involvement with their children. *Community, Work & Family*, *15*(3), 273-91.

126   Kabat-Zinn, J. (2003). Mindfulness-based interventions in context: Past, present, and future. *Clinical Psychology: Science and Practice, 10*, 144-56.

127   Johnson, P. (1964). Creative Crafts. *Childhood Education, 40(6)*, 292-7.

128 Gordon, T. (2000). *Parent Effective Traing: The Proven Program for Raising Responsible Children.* New York: Random House Inc.

129 Sunarty, K., Abimanyu, S., Idri, R. & Ahmad, A. (2014). The Relationship Between Positive Parenting and the Self-Reliance of the Children. *International Journal of Academic Research, 6(5),* 195-9.

130 Frick, P. J., Van Horn, Y., Lahey, B. B, Christ, M. G., Loeber, R., Hart, E. A., Tannenbaum, L. & Hanson, K. (1992). Oppositional defiant disorder and conduct disorder: A meta-analytic review of factor analyses and cross-validation in a clinic sample. *Clinical Psychology Review, 13,* 319-40. Cited in: Oana Alexandra, D. (2014). The Rational Positive Parenting Program for Child Externalizing Behaviour: Mechanisms of Change Analysis. *Journal of Evidence-Based Psychotherapies, 14(1),* 21-38.

131 McCord, J. (1991). Questioning the value of punishment. *Social Problems, 38,* 167-76. Cited in: Oana Alexandra, D. (2014). The Rational Positive Parenting Program for Child Externalizing Behaviour: Mechanisms of Change Analysis. *Journal of Evidence-Based Psychotherapies, 14(1),* 21-38.

132 Knight, N. K. (2010). *Wrinkling complexity: Concepts of identity and affiliation in humour.* In Bednarek, M. & Martin, J. R. (Eds.), *New discourse on language: Functional perspectives on multimodality, identity, and affiliation.* London: Continuum.

133 Zabriskie, R. B. & McCormick, B.P. (2003). Parent and child perspectives of family leisure involvement and satisfaction with family life. *Journal of Leisure Research, 35(2),* 163-89.

134 Bruner, J. (1996). *The culture of education.* Cambridge, MA: Harvard University Press.

135 Vygotsky, L. (1978). *Mind in society.* Cambridge, MA: Harvard University Press.

136   Dahlberg, G., Moss, P. & Pence, A. (1999). *Beyond quality in early childhood education and care: post-modern perspectives.* London: Falmer Press.

137 Rizzolatti, G. & Craighero, L. (2004). The mirror-neuron system. *Annual Review of Neuroscience, 27,* 169-92.

138 Bratton, S. & Landreth, G. (1995). Filial therapy with single parents: Effects on parental acceptance, empathy, and stress. *International Journal of Play Therapy, 4(1),* 61-80.

139 Stephens, T. (1988). Physical activity and mental health in the United States and Canada: Evidence from four population surveys. *Preventive Medicine, 17,* 35–47.

140 Fox, K. R. (1999). The influence of physical activity on mental well-being. *Public Health Nutrition: 2(3a),* 411-8.

141 Archer, S. (2004). *Pilates Fusion: Well-Being for Body, Mind, and Spirit.* San Francisco: Chronicle Books.

142 Flora, C. (2005). Mirror Mirror: Seeing yourself as others see you. *Psychology Today, 24,* 54-7.

143 Kabat-Zinn, J. (2003). Mindfulness-based interventions in context: Past, present, and future. *Clinical Psychology: Science and Practice, 10,* 144-56.

144 Meins, E., Fernyhough, C., Fradley, E. & Tuckey, M. (2001). Rethinking maternal sensitivity: Mothers' comments on infants' mental processes predict security of attachment at 12 months. *Journal of Child Psychology and Psychiatry and Allied Discipline, 42,* 637-48.

145 Kestenbaum, R., Farber, E. A. & Sroufe, L. A. (1989). Individual differences in empathy among preschoolers: Relation to attachment history. *New Directions for Child and Adolescent Development, 44,* 51–6.

146 Fisher, R. (2006). Still thinking: The case for meditation with children. *Thinking Skills and Creativity, 1,* 146-51.

147 Brinker, R.P., Seifer, R., & Sameroff, A.J. (1994). Relations among maternal stress, cognitive development, and early intervention in middle- and low-SES infants with developmental disabilities. *American Journal on Mental Retardation, 98,* 463-80.

148 Nicholls, L., Lewis, A. J., Petersen, S., Swinburn, B., Moodie, M. & Millar, L. (2014). Parental Encouragement of Healthy Behaviours: Adolescent Weight Status and Health-Related Quality of Life. *BMC Public Health, 14(1),* 1-18.

149 Izard, C. E. (2002). Translating emotion theory and research into preventive interactions. *Psychological Bulletin, 128,* 796-824.

150 Miller, A. L., Gouley, K. K., Seifer, R., Zakriski, A., Eguia, M. & Vergnani, M. (2005), Emotion Knowledge Skills in Low-income Elementary School Children: Associations with Social Status and Peer Experiences. *Social Development, 14,* 637-51.

151 Barnett, M.A. (1987). *Empathy and related responses in children.* In Eisenberg, N. & Strayer, J. (eds). *Empathy and its development.* New York: Cambridge University Press.

152 Davidov, M. & Grusec, J.E. (2006). Untangling the links of parental responsiveness to distress and warmth to child outcomes. *Child Development 77(1),* 44-58.

153 Denham, S.A. (1997). "When I have a bad dream, my Mommy holds me": Preschoolers conceptions of emotions, parental socialization, and emotional competence. *International Journal of Behavioral Development, 20,* 301-19.

154 Lieberman, M. D., Eisenberger, N. I., Crockett, M. J., Tom, S. M., Pfeifer, J. H. & Way, B. M. (2007). Putting Feelings into Words: Affect Labelling Disrupts Amygdala Activity in Response to Affective Stimuli. *Psychological Science, 18(5),* 421-8.

155 King, L. A. (2001). The Health Benefits of Writing about Life Goals. *Personality and Social Psychology Bulletin, 27(7),* 798-807.

156 Hoffman, M. L. & Saltzein, H.D. (1967). Parental discipline and the child's moral development. *Journal of Personality and Social Psychology, 5,* 5-57.

157 Dekovic, M. & Janssens, J. M. (1992). Parents' child: Rearing style and child's sociometric status. *Developmental Psychology 28(5),* 925-32.

158 Lyubomirsky, S., King, L. & Diener, E. (2005). The Benefits of Frequent Positive Affect: Does Happiness Lead to Success? *Psychological Bulletin, 131(6),* 803-55.

159 Alcoff, L. (1991). The problem of speaking for others. *Cultural Critique,* 5-32.

160 Fine, M. (1998). *Working the hyphens: reinventing self and other in qualitative research.* Cited in Page, T. (2012). A Shared Place of Discover and Creativity: Practices of Contemporary Art and Design Pedagogy. *International Journal of Art & Design Education, 31(1),* 67-77.

161 Humphrey, C. (2007) Insider-outsider: activating the hyphen, *Action Research, 5(11),* 11-26. Cited in Page, T. (2012). A Shared Place of Discover and Creativity: Practices of Contemporary Art and Design Pedagogy. *International Journal of Art & Design Education, 31(1),* 67-77.

162 Klabunde, B. (2004). *Having the Grace to Say 'Yes'.* Insight for Living.

163 Coyne, L. & Murrell, A. (2009). *The Joy of Parenting: An Acceptance and Commitment Therapy Guide to Parenting in the Early Years.* Oakland, US: New Harbinger Publications

164 Jenkins, R. (2008). *Social Identity* (3rd ed). Oxon, UK: Routledge.

165 Zambianchi, M. & Ricci Bitti, P. E. (2014). The Role of Proactive Coping Strategies, Time Perspective, Perceived Efficacy on Affect Regulation, Divergent Thinking and Family Communication in Promoting Social Well-Being in Emerging Adulthood. *Social Indicators Research, 16(2),* 493-507.

166 Gilligan, R. (2000). Adversity, resilience and young people: The protective value of positive school and spare time experiences, *Children & Society, 14*(1), 37-47.

167 Burgess, L. & Addison, N. (2007) Conditions for learning: partnerships for engaging secondary pupils with contemporary art. *International Journal of Art & Design Education, 26(2),* 185-98.

168 Strader, T. J. (2011). *Digital technology in the 21st century.* In Troy, J. S. [ed] *Digital Product Management, Technology and Practice: Interdisciplinary Perspectives.* Hershey: Business Science. Cited in Ting Wu, C. S., Fowler, C., Yin Lam, W. Y., Ting Wong, H., Man Wong, C. H. & Yuen Loke, A. (2014). Parenting approaches and digital technology use of preschool age children in a Chinese community. *Italian Journal of Pediatrics, 40(1),* 1-17.

169 Koo, C., Wati, Y., Lee, C. C. & Oh, H. Y. (2011). Internet-Addicted Kids and South Korean Government Efforts: Boot-Camp Case. *Cyber Psychology, Behavior & Social Networking, 14(6),* 391-4.

170 Widyanto, L. & McMurran, M. (2004). The psychometric properties of the Internet Addiction Test. *Cyber Psychology & Behavior, 7,* 443-50.

171 Ting Wu, C. S., Fowler, C., Yin Lam, W. Y., Ting Wong, H., Man Wong, C. H. & Yuen Loke, A. (2014). Parenting approaches and digital technology use of preschool age children in a Chinese community. *Italian Journal of Pediatrics, 40(1),* 1-17.

172 Subrahmanyam, K., Kraut, R., Greenfield, P. M. & Gross, E. F. (2000). The impact of home computer use on children's activities and development. *Future Child, 10,* 123-44.

173 Kennedy, S.S. & Mohr, W.K. (2001). The conundrum of children in the US healthcare system. *Nursing Ethics, 8(3),* 213-7.

174 Alderson, P. & Montgomery, J. (1996). *Healthcare choices: Making decisions with children.* London: Institute for Public Policy Research.